MARTIN LUTHER

AND

THE REFORMATION

MARTIN LUTHER

and

The Reformation

A. G. DICKENS

*Professor of History
in the University of London*

THE ENGLISH UNIVERSITIES PRESS LTD
ST PAUL'S HOUSE WARWICK LANE
LONDON EC4

SBN 340 05968 0

The English Universities Press Ltd
St Paul's House, Warwick Lane, London EC4

Printed and bound in Great Britain by
Hazell Watson & Viney Ltd
Aylesbury, Bucks

Introduction to the Series

This series has been undertaken in the conviction that no subject is more important than history. For though the conquests of natural science (nuclear fission, the exploration of space, genetic advance, bacteriology, etc.) have given their character to the age, it is actually a greater need to gain control of the forces of nature loosed upon us. The prime urgency, the deepest necessity is in the human field: to understand the nature and condition of man as a pre-condition of better controls, and fewer disasters, in the world of politics and society.

There is no better introduction to this sphere, and the understanding of its problems, than history. *Some* knowledge of history, we feel, ought to prevent some mistakes: at every point we can learn vicariously from the experience of others before us.

To take one point only – the understanding of politics: how can we understand the world of affairs around us, if we do not know how it came to be what it is? How to interpret the United States, or Soviet Russia, France, Germany or Britain without some knowledge of their history?

Some evidence of the growing awareness of this may be seen in the great increase of interest in history among the general public, and in the much larger place the subject has come to take in education.

The most congenial, as well as the most concrete and practical, approach to history is the biographical: through the lives of great men whose careers have been significant in history. Fashions in historical writing have their ups and downs; men's and women's lives have their perennial interest – though in this series we are chiefly concerned to show their historical significance, the contribution they made to their age: *Men and their Times*.

A generation ago historical biographies were rather unfashionable with analytical historians and technicians, like Namier: he ended by writing scores of miniature biographies of M.P.s. The detailed analysis of Civil War and Commonwealth has ended by showing that there were almost as many party-divisions as there were individuals. We are back in the realm of biography and the biographical approach to history, since there is no greater diversity, variety and subtlety than in the lives of individual men and women, particularly those who left a mark on their time.

A. L. Rowse

Oxford

Contents

Acknowledgements

I acknowledge with much gratitude the important and helpful suggestions made by the General Editor, from whose example and counsels I have so often benefited during the last thirty years. During the last stages of my work, I was most fortunate in having as visiting colleague Professor Carl S. Meyer, whose scholarship comes from the heart of the great American Lutheran tradition. I was happy to accept some twenty or more changes suggested by him. I must also thank Professors Gordon Rupp and James Atkinson, whom I did not similarly burden on this occasion, but who put me firmly on the rails when I seriously took up Luther-studies some years ago.

King's College,
Strand,
London, w.c.2.

Chapter One

Early Life

IN April 1521, immediately after defying Pope and Emperor at the Diet of Worms, Martin Luther on his return northward paid a visit to Möhra near Eisenach in Thuringia, the home of his ancestors. Within this charming area of great hills and woods he was interested to discover a whole host of Luthers— or Luders, as the name was then most commonly spelt. For centuries they had been free men and peasant-farmers, living under the mild yoke of the Saxon Electors and having hereditary rights over their miniature properties. They had kept their legal and economic status by refusing to divide their holdings and by the custom of leaving all to the youngest son. On this basis one branch of the Luder family succeeded in maintaining itself at Möhra into our present century. But the system compelled the older sons to migrate and seek their living elsewhere, and this had happened to the sons of Heine Luder, grandfather of the Reformer.

Martin's own father appears to have trained as a copper-miner while still at Möhra. Ambitious, hard-working, impulsively outspoken, he has a place of his own in the story of Luther's earlier life. He was usually known as Big Hans to distinguish him from his brother Little Hans: a desirable distinction, since even in that rough society Little Hans became notorious as a tavern-brawler and often figured in court. Soon after his marriage to Margarete Ziegler Big Hans moved out some hundred miles north-west to Eisleben, the little walled town ruled by the Counts of Mansfeld. Here on 11 November, 1483, his second son Martin was baptised and in accordance with pious custom received his name from the calendar saint of the day, who happened to be the great monastic founder, St. Martin of Tours.

In the summer of 1484 the family moved a little further on to Mansfield, the town where Martin spent his childhood. By 1491 Hans had become a shareholder in a small mining company and a respected member of one of the municipal committees, but he acquired the usual large family—four sons and four daughters were living in 1505—and life offered no superfluities during these years. Hence Martin had the advantage of belonging to a family fighting its way upwards in a hard world. In 1501 Hans saved enough to send his son to the university. Six years later he appears as a joint lessee of several mines and furnaces, and when Martin celebrated his first mass Hans rode to Erfurt with twenty companions to celebrate the event, making a handsome gift to Martin's religious community. He was ambitious for his gifted son, respectful of learning, hard-headed, hot-tempered but, as Martin recalls, mellow and amusing when well plied with drink. In later years the worn peasant-faces of Hans and his wife were to be recorded by Lucas Cranach. They look what they were: prosaic, careful, sensible people with no false pretensions. Their religious background was wholly unremarkable, though in her final years at least Margarete had a reputation for piety. Martin remembered that they sometimes beat him for minor misdemeanours, but such was then the almost universal habit of parents. Throughout his years in monastic and academic life he continued in affectionate relations with his parents; they survived in fact until 1530–31 and saw him among the most famous figures of Europe.

Among these tough and laborious people, the absence of literary habits should not imply a featureless mental life. As one might still surmise from a tour of the small towns of Thuringia and Saxony, they remained countrymen and forest-dwellers as much as burgesses. They lived very close to the spirits of nature and the pagan superstitions of pre-Christian times. Luther again recalled that his mother had to placate a local witch who caused her children pains and made them scream as if they were dying. Witchcraft was even blamed for the death of one of his little brothers. The mature Luther was less superstitious than most of his contemporaries, but even he more than half believed that demons poisoned the crops and infected cattle with the plague, that the insane were possessed by devils, that ferocious earth-spirits attacked miners underground, that Satan and his minions dragged down careless bathers in the treacherous reaches of the Elbe at Wittenberg. In later life his Protestant theology suggested that these malevolent beings had little influence over righteous men; he even doubted the general belief of Renaissance scholars that God would reveal his mysteries to the astrologers. But his youth was passed amid a cosmic warfare between the powers of darkness and light. The saints were helpers in need; in particular the kindly cults of the Blessed Virgin and of St. Anne, patroness of miners, brought safety and prosperity.

Throughout all Europe around 1500 the images of saints, their altars, festivals and fraternities occupied a central place in the popular religion. Their legends and anniversaries made the Christian year a colourful jungle; their acts of healing and protection were sought by prayers, vows and contributions to shrines. They, and most of all the Virgin Mary, were intermediaries pleading the cause of poor, sinning humanity before an inconceivably terrible God. Both the Father and the Son were seen first and foremost as the Judges of mankind. Luther's early image of Christ derived from a painting he saw in a church: it showed the Saviour sitting on a rainbow judging the world. As a young man he fully shared both the fear of Christ and the corresponding reliance upon the saints. "St Anne was my idol and St. Thomas my apostle." When in his friary he saw the picture of Jesus he would cast down his eyes in fear; often, he relates, his prayer took the form: "Dear Mary, pray to your Son for me and still his anger." This terror before an august God was no twist of an abnormal mind. Such notions beset many of those more sensitive and honest spirits who could not, like the materialist mass of mankind, separate life from belief, give frequent rein to instinct, hope that some kindly saint might be induced to snatch them at the last moment from the jaws of Gehenna.

Apart from these common mental discomforts, Martin Luther's childhood and adolescence pursued a remarkably settled course. In the school at Mansfeld he began Latin, though as yet he can hardly have progressed to the ancient and universally-employed grammar of Donatus, which in later life he warmly commended. Here, and for that matter when he came to use Donatus at Eisenach, he probably handled no books of his own, but would follow the normal practice of writing down dictated passages to learn by rote. This drudgery formed the basis of the feats of memorisation displayed by him and by so many of his fellow theologians and philosophers. On the other hand, he later regretted that he had been taught no history at school, while his lack of formal instruction in mathematics made this a weak subject throughout his life. Latin and music were the essential components of a curriculum mainly designed to produce clerics; they went hand-in-hand with religious instruction, since the boys had to sing daily in church and thereby learned not only the elements of music but the ancient Creeds, the Commandments, the *Te Deum*, the Latin hymns and the whole text of the mass. Like most others of the period, Luther's teachers flogged their pupils for failure to learn, the senior boys even for talking German during school-hours. Like other eminent men of the time, he recollected with contempt the slow learning and the heavy-handed discipline then current everywhere.

Another common feature of the system was the semi-vagrant schoolboy tramping off to some other town far from home, helped on perhaps by fortuitous charity or dependent on the good offices of a distant kinsman or family friend. Full of physical and moral dangers, this world doubtless bred resource and self-reliance. Luther entered it at the age of fourteen, when he went in charge of an older boy to the grammar school at Magdeburg, one of the great cities of Germany. A major centre of trade in corn, wool and cloth, with a cathedral and a vast array of churches and monasteries, it must have presented a remarkable contrast to the little mining towns of Martin's earlier experience. During his year there he almost certainly attended the school conducted by the Brethren of the Common Life. This order of laymen, for which Luther was to maintain a high regard, cultivated a semi-monastic discipline and had spread across northern Europe since its foundation in the Netherlands a century earlier by the mystic Geert Groot. Its quakerish pietism had been given a permanent memorial in the famous *Imitatio Christi* of Thomas à Kempis (d. 1471) long before Luther encountered it at Magdeburg.

Here, many years before he began to see its meaning, he breathed the atmosphere of the *devotio moderna*, the 'new' religious sensibility which was to provide one of the psychological bases for the Protestant Reformation. The Brethren and many like-minded men and women valued spiritual 'experiences' and undertook methodical contemplation. They had progressed beyond the popular saint-cults but at the same time they regarded academic theology and philosophy as broken reeds, as exercises of vain curiosity, as furnishing no reliable paths to the knowledge of God. While in this sense anti-intellectual, the *devotio* did not seek to dispense with book-learning. To their assiduous study of mystical literature, the Brethren united a sound classical tradition. Their school at Deventer became especially famous, with Thomas à Kempis and Nicholas of Cusa among its early pupils and Erasmus (b. 1469) among those of a later generation.

The effective influence of this tradition upon Luther we should presumably ascribe to a later stage, since after a year his parents arranged for him to complete his schooling at Eisenach, a town which must have been well known to them before they emigrated from nearby Möhra. Overshadowed by the romantic castle of the Wartburg, it had traditions of courtly life dating back to the days of Walther von der Vogelweide and the Minnesänger, but apart from its well-known religious houses, it had become a pleasant, provincial backwater. Luther called it his 'beloved Eisenach', though in one of his less mellow moods he dubbed it 'a nest of priests'. Here he spent three or four years preparing for the university and receiving many kindnesses not only from remote relatives but from the pious merchant-patrician families of Cotta and Schalbe, in whose homes he encountered humane and cultured habits very different from those of his own home. Meanwhile under the training of diligent, kindly, old-fashioned teachers, the youth rapidly outpaced most of his companions. He acquired the figures of

5

Latin rhetoric through that highly systematised textbook, the *Doctrinale* of Alexander of Villedieu. He came to delight in the Latin dramatists, especially Terence, of whom he later remarked that a page of the comedies was worth more than all the dialogues and colloquies of Erasmus. All this hardly amounted to classical humanism, but it gave Luther his fluent late-medieval Latin—in such hands a powerful weapon—and it awoke the outstanding linguistic capacity that enabled him in subsequent years to master both Greek and Hebrew. By the year 1501 he stood well prepared for the next stage.

The register of the university of Erfurt records in the summer term of that year the entry of 'Martinus Ludher ex Mansfelt' into the faculty of arts. Again, the change of scene must have been dramatic. The city with its frowning walls and innumerable towers not only boasted the Thuringian university but ranked with Nuremberg, Strassburg and Cologne among the most populous places in the Empire. Yet if, as claimed by Luther and others, it had some 50,000 inhabitants, probably half these lived in the country area under its rule. Erfurt had won virtual self-government from its nominal overlord the Archbishop of Mainz. Called 'Little Rome', it contained all the appurtenances of a German metropolis from the lavish churches to the well-managed municipal brothels. By the standards of that day the university itself was large and established: it dated from 1392 and was now admitting some three or four hundred freshmen every year. Luther lived in the minor college or *bursa* of St. George, known in student-parlance as 'the Beer-bag'. Its discipline was strict, rather like that of a seminary, but this would hardly oppress Luther, who worked hard at the *trivium* (grammar, logic and rhetoric) and took his bachelor's degree in eighteen months. He then pursued the *quadrivium* (music, astronomy, arithmetic and geometry) together with a liberal dosage of philosophy based on Aristotle, and he became a master of arts early in 1505. Both these degrees he obtained in the shortest time permitted by the statutes and in the list of masters he came second out of seventeen candidates. When in later years he criticised Erfurt, it was not for poor teaching but for the narrowness of its courses and its lack of true academic freedom. His professors were Jodocus Trutvetter and Bartholomäus Arnold von Usingen, both dutiful exponents of the so-called *via moderna*, the Nominalist school of philosophy based on the writings of William of Occam (d. c. 1349) and of their own master Gabriel Biel (d. 1495).

Both Luther's teachers lived on to oppose his Protestant doctrine, yet their influence (which Luther continued to encounter for the rest of his time in Erfurt) left permanent marks upon his thinking. Nominalist metaphysics meant that neither the existence of God nor the orthodox doctrine of the Trinity could be proved by man's wretched little rational arguments, but only by God's own acts of self-revelation. For the Occamists the two worlds of philosophy and theology, of Aristotle and revealed religion, did not neatly conjoin, as St. Thomas Aquinas had taught. Each world operated according to its own law. The supernatural world was impenetrable to human reason; revelation must be taken on trust. In Luther's own later phrase: 'because the Holy Spirit says it is true, it is true.' From his Occamist philosophy and theology Luther derived something more than a rejection of Thomist Aristotelianism. In this *via moderna* can be seen a distinct basis for Luther's sense of the majesty, the independence, the 'otherness' of God, who in his seemingly arbitrary omnipotence could save even a man devoid of any good works or intrinsic merits.

On the other hand we shall see that Luther was to diverge widely from Occamist theology in his doctrine of human salvation. The *via moderna* had distinctly Pelagian tendencies; it still thought of man as a free agent, one able to cooperate with God, able to make himself worthy of salvation. When in later years Luther had studied Paul and Augustine he came vehemently to deny these notions. In Luther's mature view, St. Paul granted no rôle in the task of salvation to human free-will or self-betterment, accorded no saving merit whatever to human good works. To such problems we shall return in more detail, but from this first mention of Luther's contact with the *via moderna* we need to guard against fashionable but exaggerated estimates of its influence upon his mature thought. Naturally, as a mere discipline in logical analysis and method Luther's experience in

7

the schools of Erfurt had great importance for him; it constantly registers upon his mature thought and literary style. In addition he learned at Erfurt something of the current cosmology and science: that the earth is a sphere, that the moon produces the tides, that storms are (generally speaking!) produced by natural forces, that both alchemy and astrology are to be taken with a pinch of salt.

The other set of ideas current in the most progressive universities derived from the linguistic and historical studies of the humanists. Whereas Occamism destroyed the other scholastic systems with their own weapons, the humanists turned aside from the whole approach of scholasticism. Prominent in several Italian cities well before Petrarch's day, humanism in general cannot be dubbed anti-Christian. It nevertheless propounded a new way of life and thought based upon the recovery of Greek and Roman civilisation as it had really existed, not as hitherto seen through Christian scholastic eyes. And as it developed it tended to stress the dignity of man as a self-determining and even self-sufficient creature.

Luther himself was never very passionately interested in the history of pagan culture; he never tried to write Latin like Cicero; he could never begin to accept the attempts of Erasmus and others to sketch out a hybrid Christian-humanist theology. During his Erfurt years he certainly studied classical authors; then, or soon afterwards, some of his friends attended the famous circle of classicists assembled by Konrad Mudt (Mutianus) at Gotha only thirty miles away. One of these friends was Johann Jäger, (Crotus Rubeanus) the chief author of the first part of the *Epistolae Obscurorum Virorum* (1513); another was Georg Spalatin, who as chaplain to the Elector Frederick the Wise of Saxony was destined to play a vital part in enlisting that prince's support for Luther. If the future Reformer stood on the fringes of German humanism and viewed some of its elements as profoundly alien, he became a biblical theologian and as such had every inducement to utilise the best texts and the new methods of textual criticism furnished by the humanists. This he did not fail to do and in a limited sense he stands among the heirs of Erasmus and Reuchlin. Like them he desired above all to see a rebirth, but only the rebirth of one special part of the Ancient World: primitive Christianity. Having in later years renounced Rome, he never ceased to contend that his task was one of restoration, and he resented nothing more than the charge that he was inventing a new religion.

When Luther graduated as a master, such thoughts had not yet taken shape in his mind. To his proud father (who now began to address his son as *Sie* instead of using the familiar *Du*) the notion of a career as a theologian was even more unimaginable. He dreamed of marrying Martin into a family of high social standing, a step which would have excluded not only the priesthood but even a chair in the university, where lay as well as clerical teachers normally remained celibate. The obvious route to fame and fortune attracted the father. In Erfurt there flourished a large law school, and to graduates in either the civil or the canon law there opened up glittering prospects either in the law-courts or in the service of princes, bishops and cities. In later years Luther frequently disparaged the legal profession as one concerned not with truth but with sordid gain. If in 1505 he felt its attractions, this must have been momentary. He enrolled in the law school during the late spring, but by July he had repented his decision, and to the amazement of his friends and the consternation of his father he entered the house of Augustinian Friars at Erfurt.

The curious story of his decision was told by an Erfurt friend in 1519 and confirmed by Luther himself some twenty years later still. Coming from his home at Mansfeld back to Erfurt on 2 July, he was overtaken by a violent storm and a thunderbolt hurled him to the ground. In terror he called to his patroness, "Dear St. Anne, I will become a monk." In earlier times such events had not been uncommon, and in 1115 the famous Norbert, founder of the Premonstratensian Order, had been converted when similarly in danger of death during a thunderstorm. Luther also recalled, when criticising monasticism, that he had honoured this vow against his will, and he did in fact consult friends, some of whom sought to exonerate him, others to hold him to the vow.

While there seems no reason to doubt the impulsive gesture

in the thunderstorm or the subsequent brief agony of indecision, these events apparently formed the culmination of a slow change of heart. The middle-aged Luther liked to dramatise his earlier life in terms of landmarks. But at Erfurt he had been a serious and devout young man, long in contact with clerics of deep piety. In those days the challenge to enter a religious order must at some stage have been experienced by most people of his stamp. And there are some further anecdotes concerning Luther in the year 1505 which show him as sobered by untoward events into a contempt of the world. In the plague that swept parts of Germany during that summer he had lost several friends and even, according to some stories, two of his own brothers. Again, only a few weeks before the thunderstorm he had stumbled upon his sword while out walking near Erfurt, had severed a leg-artery and lay in much danger until a surgeon hastened out from the city to administer first-aid. Whatever the importance of all these incidents, Luther's hesitation was brief and his ultimate decision firm. On 16 July he held a farewell-party, with music and some female company. The following day a group of depressed comrades accompanied him through the streets and saw him disappear behind the great gates of the Augustinian Eremites.

Since its foundation in the thirteenth century this house had outgrown in size and wealth the other local mendicant houses. Many of its novices came from distinguished families and all were subjected to careful tests of vocation. At the time of Luther's entry it had a membership of more than seventy friars, some of whom taught theology in the university or preached in the city churches. It was one of the thirty houses of Eremites in the Saxon-Thuringian province of the Order that had been led into the strict observance, as distinct from the laxer 'conventual' discipline of the rest. The district vicar of this observant group of houses was the Saxon nobleman Johann von Staupitz, a distinguished writer and spiritual counsellor in the mystical tradition of the *devotio moderna*. At this time Staupitz planned to draw all the Saxon houses into the observance and he cooperated to this end with the Italian leader of that movement, the famous classicist and hebraist Giles of Viterbo, who soon afterwards became head of the whole Order.

In the Erfurt house the discipline appears to have been quite rigorous during Luther's novitiate. He prayed and slept in a tiny cell which lacked any form of heating and overlooked the burial-place of the friars. The long round of private devotions and chapel-services was broken by frequent examination and confession, while the rule of silence was strictly enforced in chapel, cell and refectory. Luther had to take his turn with the menial sanitary duties and in begging for alms, though in the case of this well-endowed house begging had become a personal discipline rather than a necessity. His enthusiasm carried him through the novitiate with such success that in his case the customary year was somewhat shortened. During the years which followed he proved a devout and strenuous friar, winning excellent opinions from his superiors. "I experienced in myself", he wrote later on, "how tranquil Satan was wont to be in the first years of monkhood", and again, "If ever a monk could have got to heaven through monkery, I would have done it. To this all my monastic friends who know me will testify." The harsh criticisms of cloister-life made by Luther the Reformer do not represent the thoughts of young Luther in the cloister. And even these criticisms are not directed against his former superiors, whom he continued to respect, but rather against a whole system which severely punished minor slips in ritual and discipline while failing to check pride, hatred, laziness and real sins, both spiritual and carnal.

After the first and simpler phase of monastic life, Luther became subject to those terrifying attacks of fear and depression which in varying forms beset him throughout life.

They lasted, to be sure, only a short time, but they were so hard and infernal that no tongue can express and no pen describe their power, nor can anyone believe it who has never had the experience. Should they remain at their highest point for an hour, yes, only the tenth part of an hour, the victim must needs perish and all his bones be reduced to ashes.

They were accompanied by a conviction that he was hated by

God and destined to fail in his personal search for salvation. "My heart shivered and trembled as to how God could be merciful to me." During these *Anfechtungen*, confession and penance afforded at most a temporary relief. And when he turned to the Bible Luther could see only the Christ on the rainbow judging all men, not Christ the Lamb of God taking away the sins of the world. The old slander that Luther was a mere misfit, troubled about actual sins of the flesh, has long been abandoned, even by his severer critics. Such fears as his were then widely shared under the impact of distorted concepts of God: Luther's case was exceptional mainly through his utter honesty, his refusal of the spiritual opiates which satisfied men of less acute sensibility. To this sense of the awful contrast between fallen man and the demands of an inconceivably pure and resplendent Deity, he ultimately found a theological solution in the doctrine of justification by faith alone. But even when he had learned to throw himself with confidence on the unearned mercy of the Redeemer, Luther occasionally suffered new *Anfechtungen*, provoked by a sense of his failure to regenerate popular religion or by the fear that his revolt might after all have been mistaken, a road to perdition for millions. These later attacks he himself supposed to have been physically conditioned, and their precise relationship with the early attacks in the monastery remains obscure.

Today it is fatally easy to select the most obvious label from the textbook of psychiatric medicine, and to call Luther a manic-depressive throughout the whole course of his life. But on closer inspection his mental history does not conform to the usual patterns of this neurosis. At no stage did the attacks hamper work demanding extreme concentration. In the cloister he was successfully learning Greek and Hebrew with little or no guidance outside the poor textbooks then available. In later life he emerged swiftly from every attack to face tasks of immense difficulty, curiously strengthened and energetic. Even when in his spiritual abysses Luther was no mere 'patient', no ordinary sufferer answering to the modern formulae. Given the findings of psychiatry, it was inevitable that attempts would be made to explain not only his problems but also his religious and ethical convictions upon the basis of maladjustment in child-hood. The most impressive analysis of this type, Dr. Erikson's *Young Man Luther*, finds the origin of Luther's revolt in an effort to win independence from his parents and to become a person in his own right. The adolescent Luther creates a God in the image of his own irascible father, shifts his obedience to this terrible Deity and releases the venom of his defiance against the Pope. Again, Luther is caned for speaking German in school-hours, so he becomes fanatically attached to the German language. Likewise, his resentment against the severity of his mother causes him to dethrone the Virgin Mary.

Such hypotheses while hard to prove are also hard to dis-prove, and historians should curb their own tendency to laugh out of court the contributions of a science which they imper-fectly understand. Even so, in Luther's case we feel bound to indicate some factual obstacles. This type of theory seems to base Luther's career upon three or four sentences, selected from the late and unreliable *Table Talk*, to the exclusion of much competing or contradictory evidence. When interpreted in the light of contemporary manners, Luther's childhood and adoles-cence seem strikingly 'normal' and unsensational. By the stand-ards expected in that period, his parents were far from heavy-handed; they were deeply devoted to his welfare and he re-mained on unusually affectionate terms with them to the end of their long lives. Luther needed no irascible father to provide him with the image of an angry and inscrutable God, for on every side orthodox theologians and popular beliefs provided such an image. And in the actual event his attack on the Pope brought him no 'release' but only further torment. So far as concerns his alleged complex over the German language, in fact he became just as voluble and prolific in Latin as in German; his Bible-reading and private devotions were carried out in the former. While on his revolt he sought to abolish saint-worship, he did not in actual fact single out the Blessed Virgin, but continued to regard her with a heartfelt reverence quite unusual among Protestants. Altogether, so far from undertaking his revolt in an ambitious spirit of self-fulfilment, both he and

13

his friends often feared, and with good reason, that his enterprise would be rewarded by a swift martyrdom.

No arbitrary selection of fragments from such a body of evidence can form a reliable substitute for data drawn by a skilled diagnostician. Emphatically, this patient is not lying on the clinical couch! We are dealing here with one of the most extraordinary men of history, a man whose creativity was even more remarkable than his neuroses. Even if, despite all the objections, we proclaim this evidence enough to justify a diagnosis, we end by 'explaining' singularly little about Luther's enormous achievement, his amazing energy and versatility, his immense and lasting impact upon the German people, upon the Christian world. There have been hosts of manic-depressives, many young men subject to identity-crises, yet there has been only one Luther. A mere manic-depressive is not led by his psychiatric problems into propounding and setting forth with demonic energy a system of ideas which tears a whole civilisation asunder and alters the course of western history. No less than this Luther was to accomplish.

Chapter Two

The Formative Years

LUTHER'S troubled phases may have bulked less large in the life of the young friar than in the recollections of the ageing ecclesiastical statesman. Certainly his monastic life formed a period of intense and absorbing intellectual labour. His novitiate over, he prepared for ordination by a close study of Gabriel Biel's famous work on the mass, which covered not only the appropriate theology but the practical details needed by the celebrant. The onus imposed upon the priest deeply affected Luther, and when on 2 May 1507 he celebrated his first mass he suffered a sense of terror in thus presuming to address God. Having passed through the minor orders, he had been ordained priest about a month earlier, and the date of his mass had been appointed by the friary to suit the convenience of Hans Luther and the twenty friends who rode over from Mansfeld. Doubtless for Martin this was a happy event, but even now his hardheaded father remained unconvinced that he had chosen aright. It was probably on this occasion that, in answer to some remark that Martin had been drawn to the cloister by a heavenly vision, Hans replied, "I hope it was no illusion and trick of the Devil". When afterwards Martin came to dedicate his work *On Monks' Vows* to his father, he recalled these blunt words and added, "It drove roots into my heart, as though God were speaking through your mouth".

If at this moment Luther really felt misgivings, the succeeding period of theological study can have left him little time to indulge them. His Order was intent to make the best use of its men and to train university theologians to the best of its considerable resources. At Erfurt a master of arts proceeding to theology embarked upon a further five years' study to reach the degree of *baccalaureus biblicus*. Then for two years the bachelor prepared lectures on two books of the Bible, one from each Testament, under the close supervision of a doctor of divinity. The student-lecturer next became a *sententiarius*, entitled to lecture under closely prescribed limits upon the great twelfth-century textbook of scholastic theology, the *Sentences* of Peter Lombard. When he had successfully expounded two books of this work, he was entitled *baccalaureus formatus* and spent a further two years in preaching, disputation and exegesis. This done, and a lengthy disputation duly executed before the whole faculty, he could supplicate for his doctorate in theology. He had at last reached the top of a long and slippery ladder from which many candidates fell during the ascent. If doctors were relatively few in number and commonly attained high office or influence, they had at least earned these privileges by sheer tenacity.

Besides the *Sentences*, the commentaries available to Luther included the *Collectorium* of Gabriel Biel, the *Quaestiones* by William of Occam and those by Pierre d'Ailly. He had not to unlearn his arts studies now he came to theology, since these books were all in the same Nominalist tradition. Luther interpreted the *Sentences* through these spectacles, not through the ones furnished by the *Summa Theologica* of Thomas Aquinas. But the contention of Luther's critics that he never encountered the classics of the high middle ages seems contradicted by the knowledge of Aquinas, Scotus and Hales which he displays incidentally in his later writings. In other words, his scholastic equipment may not have been well balanced, yet in the end it was not unilateral. In Luther's day it was not incumbent upon any student, let alone upon an Augustinian, to accord the Thomist system that primacy later demanded by the Counter Reformation. Moreover, one should not impugn his studies in the supposition that the Bible suffered neglect during the later middle ages. From his cloister-days Luther seems to have possessed his own copy of the Vulgate. However divergent from Luther's mature conclusions, the official biblical teaching at least gave him a close knowledge of the Latin text and encouraged him to memorise long passages.

In the autumn of 1508 his superiors sent him to the Augustinian house at Wittenberg in order to strengthen the teaching at the university founded there only six years earlier by Frederick the Wise, Elector of Saxony. The recorded views of several contemporary visitors stress the poverty and dullness of the little Electoral town. Luther's first impressions of the place he was destined to make famous seem to have been no more favourable. At various times he expressed astonishment that Wittenberg had ever been made the seat of a university, and he spoke of it as lying "on the very borderland of civilisation". It lay on the sandy plain alongside the Elbe; its population is recorded as rising from 2,148 in 1500 to 2,453 in 1550, but Dresden itself was not much bigger and Meissen probably less. As a reminder of its colonial origins, there lay to the north and east a large unbroken Wendish population, still despised by the Germans and debarred from full citizenship. The origins of Wittenberg University owed much to the division of Saxony (1485) between the Ernestine and Albertine branches of the House of Wettin. The former had been assigned the Electorate, the lands north of the Elbe and most of Thuringia; the latter were called Dukes of Saxony and took the territories around Dresden, Leipzig and Meissen. Frederick the Wise, jealous of the fame of the century-old University of Leipzig, spared no pains to create his own northern Athens. But in order to cut the cost he mobilised the few religious foundations at Wittenberg together with their appropriated parishes to provide emoluments for the theological faculty. Besides rebuilding his own castle with its collegiate church of All Saints, he erected two major college buildings and agreed to rebuild the Augustinian cloister, the old chapel of which reminded Luther's friend Myconius of the stable at Bethlehem.

Since his accession to the Electorate in 1486 Frederick had assembled a huge collection of holy relics and had obtained from Rome special indulgences for contrite pilgrims coming to inspect them; all to such purpose that Wittenberg could now claim to be the chief centre of pilgrimage throughout north Germany. A list of the relics compiled in 1509 shows 5,005 items, including a part of the holy cradle, fragments of hay and straw from the manger, the swaddling clothes, 33 fragments of the holy cross, part of Moses' burning bush and no less than 204 assorted portions of the Holy Innocents slaughtered by Herod. Since the Elector's interest in his collection was more than merely financial, it seems one of the ironies of history that his fame derives solely from the protection he extended to the arch-enemy of such cults.

Like some new universities of our day, Wittenberg strove to attract distinguished teachers from other institutions, and while some of the recruits put up with its lack of social and scholarly amenities, others drifted away after a short period of service. In a spirit of liberalism both Realists and Nominalists were brought in to teach philosophy and theology. Among the former was Andreas Carlstadt, among the latter Luther's old professor Trutvetter, who had migrated from Erfurt the year before Luther did so. Another 'progressive' feature of Wittenberg lay in its early provision for the teaching of Greek. This feature was to attract Reuchlin's great-nephew Philip Schwarzerd, hellenised as Melanchthon, whose fame rapidly became second only to that of Luther; and it vastly improved the capacities of Wittenberg as a centre of biblical studies. Much hectic advertising and cutting of fees had at first brought in a fair number of students, but disillusion—the common reward of universities which inflate their claims—had already set in when Luther arrived: in that year only some 68 new students matriculated. He had nevertheless to carry a heavy load of teaching in moral philosophy and to continue his own studies in theology. As yet he saw little of his own superior Staupitz, who had gone to teach in Wittenberg but is known to have been absent throughout most of Luther's first visit. Another possible advantage was snatched from him by the shortness of his stay. In its anxiety to make friends and recruit staff, Wittenberg allowed such men faster advancement. Luther immediately became a *baccalaureus biblicus* and was about to be promoted *sententiarius* when in October 1509 another unexpected order recalled him to the more sober tempo of Erfurt.

Returning to the big city, he found it in political uproar. Years of declining trade and high taxation had provoked the artisans and poorer citizens—supported to some extent by the remote Elector of Mainz—against the oligarchy and the city council. The pattern was not uncommon in the towns of Reformation Europe, but in this case riot and bloodshed occupied the whole year 1510, while on the fringes there continued the endemic struggle of town against gown. In one episode the students clashed with the city guard and in response a crowd of citizens attacked various university buildings, burning the Old College with its library. This was Luther's first close contact with the mob-violence which he hated so profoundly and was often to denounce with immeasurable anger. Like countless similar affairs, it serves to remind us of the turbulence of the society amid which he worked, together with that consequent fear of chaos which haunted the minds of 'responsible' men.

During these events Luther was beginning his lectures at Wittenberg on the *Sentences*. In the city library at Zwickau there survive copies of the latter and of the minor works of St. Augustine, both containing marginal notes appended by Luther at this stage of his studies. As usual his writing is small, neat, regular, the very last hand one would connect with an exuberant personality. These notes of 1509–11 are the earliest evidences of his independent thinking. They show that he had begun to study Greek and Hebrew: they also contain classical allusions suggesting mild influences from the humanists at Erfurt and Wittenberg. In another place Luther violently attacks the famous humanist Wimpfeling, who had offended his *esprit de corps* by pointing out that St. Augustine was neither a monk nor the founder of the Augustinian Order. More seriously, he is here already encountering the most knotty problems of Christian theology, those of grace, free will and predestination, together with what became for him the central problem of all: justification, the attainment by man of a right and saving relationship with God. These marginalia show him venerating Augustine and denouncing the 'whole stupid philosophy' of the Thomists and Scotists. Along with Augustine, he is already saying that salvation is entirely the work of God, and that by his natural powers man cannot contribute anything toward the result. Co-operation with the divine will becomes possible only if man's will is first renewed by divine grace.

This phase coincided with Luther's visit to Rome, the particulars of which emerge from later statements, often made on polemical occasions and to be taken with caution. Even the dating is not quite certain, but the winter of 1510–11 seems more probable than the following winter. The dispute which took him to Rome has been only in part clarified. It concerned the plans of Staupitz for the Saxon province of the Order, and these involved the annexing of its 'conventual' houses to the observant group. This wholesale union of the province seemed to Erfurt and other observant houses to threaten the integrity of their movement and to limit their own freedom of action in winning over houses outside Saxony. The scheme was opposed also by other interests, including the city council of Nuremberg, which did not want to see its local houses placed under Staupitz, the Saxon Provincial. Luther cannot have known the ropes at Rome, and it is supposed that he went only as travelling-companion to a colleague, possibly an experienced friar from Nuremberg, charged to negotiate on behalf of the dissentient houses for leave to appeal to the Papal Curia. Though in the event permission was refused, Staupitz himself dropped his plan in 1512, and this attempted appeal to Rome by his adversaries did not affect his friendly personal relations with Luther.

Martin's impressions on the journey and in Rome were much those which one would expect from a pious German friar. When he had crossed the passes and first saw the romantic lemon trees bearing ripe and green fruit together, it reminded him how Christ provides that one defender of the faith shall ever be at hand to succeed another. The olive trees growing amid the stones recalled familiar passages in the Psalms and Gospels. Reaching the diocese of Milan, he was duly staggered by the strangeness of the Ambrosian Missal, which prevented him from saying mass there. In Florence he admired the excellent organisation of the Foundling Hospital. Throughout Italy and especially in Rome he was shocked by the evidence of treachery, blasphemy, unbelief and unnatural vices—quite apart from the uncivilised manner in which people performed the functions of nature at the street corners! Like other German pilgrims he was surprised at the number of ignorant Italian priests unable to speak tolerable Latin, and appalled by the speed with which they celebrated mass. But these modern imperfections did not spoil the ancient magic, and when he first gazed on the city he threw himself on the ground, crying "Hail, sacred Rome, sanctified by the holy martyrs in whose blood thou wast bathed". And many years afterwards he described himself as running through all the churches and shrines like a crazy saint, adding, "I believed every filthy lie I was told". But as he crawled up the Scala Sancta saying paternosters for his grandfather Heine Luder, the doubt already hammered in his mind: "Who knows whether all this is true?" He seems to have taken little interest in the new works of Renaissance Rome; after the inevitable Catacombs, the Pantheon, the Colosseum and the Baths of Diocletian attracted him most. His unfavourable impressions provided material for anti-Roman feeling long afterwards, but it seems most unlikely that they had much to do with his revolt against papal authority. He went to Rome a pious Catholic and as such he returned. As late as 1519 he was still saying that the incompetence and the sins of particular popes provide no justification for severing ourselves from the holy Church of Rome, sanctified by the blood of the Christian martyrs.

Shortly after his return, Luther left Erfurt for good, being sent back to the 'Black Cloister' of Wittenberg. The move may possibly have been due to disagreements with his Erfurt brethren springing from his continued friendship with Staupitz. The latter was now generally in Wittenberg and from 1511 dates their intimate friendship and the efforts of Staupitz to soothe the spiritual scruples and torments which beset Luther. Soon after the latter's arrival in the shabby little Electoral capital, Staupitz ordered him to apply for his doctorate and to become, somewhat against his will, a preacher. In May 1512 he attended the Augustinian chapter at Cologne and found himself nominated sub-prior of Wittenberg. In the autumn, his fees paid by the Elector, he not only took his doctorate but was promoted to membership of the university senate and to the chair of biblical theology hitherto occupied by Staupitz himself. That one so young should attain this promotion caused general surprise. Yet despite his own misgivings he soon acquired high local repute as a popular preacher in Wittenberg and its neighbourhood. Throughout all Germany preaching took place on a large scale long before the Reformation, and many thousands of sermons had already been published during the few decades between the general expansion of printing and Luther's day. Their excessive use of far-fetched allegories and their immense length must have repelled some of the laity, yet sermons were well attended in the main centres of population. Time was to show that the pulpit could become a most powerful instrument in the hands of religious reformers, innovators and cranks alike.

Luther's early Wittenberg lectures—important since they provide genuine contemporary evidence on the unfolding of his thought—have survived partly in his own hand, partly in those of his students. There are four complete courses, on *Psalms* (1513–15), *Romans* (1515–16), *Galatians* (1516–17), and *Hebrews* (1517–18). In addition, some important clues appear in certain sermons written during these same years and in a second, uncompleted course on *Psalms* (1518–19). This stage of Luther's life saw the gradual fashioning of his doctrine of justification by faith alone, the key-doctrine around which the Protestant Reformation was to turn. Nothing in Luther's thought is so crucial as this solifidianism, and whatever our interest or lack of interest in theology, we are bound to accept the fact that Luther and most contemporary intellectuals, together with a growing element among the half-educated, took the subject very seriously indeed. To study Luther without understanding his doctrine of justification would be as blind as to study Lenin without acquiring some notion of Marxism.

That Christians are justified through faith in Christ's work, not through their own good deeds, works or those of others, this is a doctrine as old as Christianity itself. Repeated again and again by St. Paul, elaborated by St. Augustine and innumerable followers, it was orthodox Catholic doctrine, even though increasingly overlaid during the medieval centuries by the emphasis of institutional and popular religion upon the rôle of good works alongside faith.

From one angle Luther can be seen as the culminating stage

of a reaction toward Augustine already in the fourteenth century observable in Gregory of Rimini (d. 1358; a General of Luther's own Order) and in two famous Englishmen, Archbishop Bradwardine and John Wycliffe. During the fifteenth century a number of these 'Reformers before the Reformation' had arisen from the background of the *devotio moderna*. John of Wesel (d. 1481), a former rector of Erfurt, had stressed strict Augustinian principles and rejected indulgences, the most debatable sort of good works. Having also questioned transubstantiation and exalted the Bible as the sole authority of faith, John had been forced to recant in 1479 and sentenced to lifelong confinement. About the same time the monastic founder John Pupper of Goch, basing his position on similar Augustinian orthodoxy, had accused his critics of Pelagianism and called Aquinas the prince of error. Meanwhile the Dutch theologian Wessel Gansfort (d. 1489) not only attacked the whole theory of indulgences but boldly disputed the power of the Pope and of the priesthood to take part in the forgiveness of sins. Albeit with far more moderation, Luther's own Order and his spiritual counsellor Staupitz maintained this tradition, despite the fact that Augustine stood diametrically opposed to the Pelagian tendency of Occamist theology.

Independently in France, the famous humanist Jacques Lefèvre of Étaples was pressing the Augustinian viewpoint with no little courage, especially in his recent edition (1512) of the Pauline Epistles. He pronounced the Bible 'the sole rule of Christians', declared divine grace the only source of salvation, and called good works merely 'the outward sign of a justifying faith'. He even doubted the sacrificial character of the mass and anticipated the Protestants by stressing its memorial character. Lefèvre also forestalled Luther in denying that monasticism was a superior vocation, and he urged that penance became harmful if it led men to trust in their own works of satisfaction. By 1520 the conservative doctors of the Sorbonne made Paris intolerable for Lefèvre and his friends.

Martin Luther thus shared a fund of ideas with many predecessors, yet they seem to have had little direct influence on him during his formative years. By 1522 he was claiming Gansfort as a precursor, yet his remarks make it quite clear that Gansfort had come to his notice recently and had not prompted his revolutionary actions. He differed from all these men in practical opportunity, in boldness of character, in readiness to envisage radical changes, in the literary genius which made the issues clear to laymen. Moreover, Luther's doctrinal theology also went significantly further than theirs. He was not satisfied merely to shift from Occamism to Augustinianism. If he had merely continued to echo Augustine, it would have been more difficult to pin charges of heresy upon him. In what respects did his teaching go beyond that of Augustine? And exactly at what stage did he take this further step?

Concerning these basic problems of his development, Luther's own recollections prove less illuminating than might have been hoped. He often refers to the helpful counsels of Staupitz, who bade him cease his self-torment and believe firmly in the forgiveness of sin through reliance on Christ. But this guidance did not solve his whole problem, and he claims to have experienced, while subsequently musing in the tower of his friary, a sudden insight of his own. Through this famous 'tower-experience' he came to a true interpretation of the phrase 'the righteous shall live by faith'. At this stage, he adds, "I broke through". So far, so good, but his account fails either to date this experience or even to recall exactly how at that moment he would have defined the act of justification. Some scholars have placed the event as early as 1513 or 1514; some have even supposed that it marked no radical departure from Augustine, even though his insight may have seemed new to Luther himself.

There seem, however, good reasons for questioning both these views. The present writer finds more convincing the arguments of the scholars who claim that Luther's ultimate doctrine was really new, and that he did not teach it until late in 1518. He was no novice, but very well read in St. Augustine, a member of the Order which was specially dedicated to upholding the doctrines of that great Father. Is he likely so to have dramatised as new any mere re-statement of Augustine's doctrine? Again, his description of the 'tower-experience' strongly suggests that it involved his mature teaching on justification. Had it taken him less far, he would hardly have signalised it as the 'break-through'. This being so, we are led to ask three more questions. What exactly did Augustine teach on justification? What was the mature teaching of Luther, as seen in his later theological works? When precisely does this mature teaching begin to show itself in the sequence of Luther's works? The answers lately suggested by the Finnish-American theologian Dr. Uuras Saar-nivaara seem to the present writer exceptionally undogmatic and respectful toward the evidence.

For Augustine, a man is indeed justified and saved by God's grace alone, and through his faith, yet the process is a gradual process of renewal, of cleansing, of healing, a process which makes a chosen man more righteous. When God has once chosen him and initiated this process, the man's refurbished will can at least cooperate with divine grace. With this Augus-tinian concept Luther began, yet his mature works introduce a very different interpretation of the original Pauline texts. This may be roughly summarised as follows. Christ alone has pre-pared the righteousness which God bestows on the men he chooses. A chosen man is not justified by any gradual and un-completed process; he is wholly and instantly justified, in Luther's characteristic phrase, 'not by pieces but in a heap'. The man is justified by the imputation—the reckoning to his credit —of this righteousness, this pardon earned for him by Christ alone. He is not merely given a gradual infusion of grace to enable him to work his passage. He is at once justified when by faith he appropriates and receives this imputed righteousness. His faith does not justify because it is a new quality in the man, but merely because it relies on God's mercy and Christ's achievement. It remains true that Luther did not wholly jetti-son Augustine's gradual process of cleansing. This he calls 'the second justification', adding that he would rather call it 'sanc-tification'. He thinks of it as a second-stage action in the soul of a man *already justified* by Christ's imputed righteousness. But a man's good works avail not at all to justify or save him; such works will surely appear as the fruits of justification, but never among its causes.

The primary element of Luther's entire theology is therefore a wholesale remission made solely by the merits of Christ's work and reckoned to the credit of the trusting sinner. In 1518 this carried immense practical implications. Most obviously, it struck at indulgences, saint-worship, shrines and pilgrimages, paid masses, the religion of outward observances and cash-payments. Moreover, it needed to be presented with skill and authority, since it squared with man-made notions of free will and justice even less readily than Augustine's scheme had done. Whatever austere theologians might say, the popular religion acted on the assumption that man, duly aided by grace, could pull himself upward by prayers, by acts of beneficence, by con-stant access to the sacraments. Within this system of 'works', the purchase of indulgences occupied a peculiar position. It was officially maintained that, through the superabundant merits of Christ and the saints, the Church could remit the temporal penalties for sin in the cases of those penitents who in contrition bought indulgences. But all too easily, this well-meaning doc-trine could degenerate into the notion that the Church was forgiving sin itself in return for a cash-payment. Simple people and over-enthusiastic preachers of indulgences both contributed to this confusion. In 1476 Pope Sixtus IV had confused the issue still further by extending the benefits of an indulgence even to souls in purgatory, and many a loving spirit clutched at this chance to shorten the purgatorial sufferings of a dead parent or child.

A less presumptuous yet still comparable reliance on 'works' arose from the foundation of chantries and other endowments for requiem masses, which had proliferated throughout Europe between the thirteenth century and Luther's day. Even educated men believed that by celebrating great numbers of such masses, the destiny of a soul would be alleviated. This claim that Christ's sacrifice could be multiplied to benefit individuals was in due course to be denounced by reformed Catholicism, but meanwhile it naturally attracted both rich patrons and impecu-nious priests. For example, King Henry VII of England ordered by will that ten thousand masses should be said for him during the month after his death, each at a fee of six pence payable to the officiating priest. In addition the King left great sums for a perpetual round of masses and prayers. This is but an extreme example of the medieval trend which, despite the minority-protest we have mentioned, had steadily run counter to the emphases of Paul and Augustine, emphases which Luther was about to develope into forms still more rigorous and still less allowing of procrastination and compromise. Armed with these considerations we may now examine Luther's early writings in chronological order, noting his development of this central issue, together with a few other related points of interest.

In the first lecture-course on *Psalms* he clearly remains under the spell of Augustine, regarding man's justification as a gradual healing from the disease of sin by the power of grace. The believer is always sinning, yet always striving toward righteousness, which he cannot fully attain in this life. Man still *becomes* righteous; he does not simply appropriate the unearned bounty of Christ's righteousness. These lectures also fail to foreshadow Luther's mature views on the revolutionary change from the 'Old Law' of Israel to the 'New Law' of the Christian Gospel. In his own later words, he makes no distinction between Moses and Christ, 'except as to time and perfection'. In view of such features, most modern authorities would reject the theory that Luther's 'tower-experience' could have taken place in these years 1513–15. Yet one notes with interest that the lectures on *Psalms* show Luther using as his chief modern commentary the *Psalterium Quintuplex* published in 1509 by Lefèvre of Étaples.

Luther's next course, that on *Romans*, shows not only an advancing Augustinianism but a close acquaintance with the recent Greek New Testament of Erasmus (1516) and also with those German mystics upon whom the *devotio moderna* had been based. While lecturing on *Romans* he had been reading on the advice of Staupitz the sermons of Johann Tauler (d. 1361): more important, he also read the famous little treatise *A German Theology*, in his day wrongly attributed to Tauler. This book Luther actually edited and published in 1516, adding an appreciative introduction of his own. It was his first work to be printed. These mystics harmonised with his present mood. They too had little use for human merit and its rewards; still less for an externalised religion of observances. They demanded humility, self-examination and self-condemnation; they argued the necessity for anguish and fear, for experience of conversion and ultimate trust. In them Luther could find the reassuring notion that spiritual affliction and testing should be interpreted as signs of divine favour. As Luther worked on the crucial passages in *Romans*, he found some congenial and pertinent ideas in the mystics, but such ideas were not destined in fact to lie at the heart of his mature message. Luther was essentially a biblical theologian searching for the truth in the written record, in the biblical manifestation of the Word of God. He was not a mystic; he did not seek to work his way by the traditional techniques of self-abandonment up a ladder of 'experiences' from the lower to the higher 'states'. Unlike that of the mystics, his message was to be christocentric, based on objective evidence, essentially historical. It concerned itself neither with the neo-Platonist abstractions beloved of many mystics, nor with the quest for 'states' which (as we now know) have been shared by non-Christians. It was not optimistic, but tragic : a *theologia crucis*. It began and ended with the blood and sweat of a real man who shared and overcame all men's terrors, physical and spiritual, upon the cross.

In *Romans* Luther encountered not only the earliest masterpiece of Christian theology but the most sustained biblical treatment of the problem of justification. He boldly called it the most important book of the New Testament. In certain passages of the lectures on *Romans* he approaches nearer toward his final teaching. He denies, for example, the mystical doctrine that in the depth of his soul man has an inherent spark of righteousness. Luther stresses that the whole movement comes from outside, from divine grace. He nevertheless continues to echo Augustine's gradualist concept of justification, and when he uses the word imputation, he gives it a far less absolute sense than in his later works. This can also be said of his lectures on *Galatians* and on *Hebrews* and of his first independent book, an explanation of the Seven Penitential Psalms, published early in 1517. But in another respect these writings ranging from 1516 to the early months of 1518 do mark a real departure from Augustine. He now upholds the literal interpretation of the

Scriptures and seeks to abandon the old 'fourfold method' (literal, figurative, moral and anagogical) of scriptural exegesis. Yet this protest against the over-elaborate allegorising of the schoolmen cannot claim entire novelty; in substance it had already been made, not only by recent critics like Reuchlin and Erasmus, but two centuries earlier by the great Parisian scholar Nicholas of Lyra (d. 1340), whose works were still being widely read and were well known to Luther.

In April 1518 Luther drew up some theses for a chapter of the German Augustinian houses at Heidelberg, and while these contain some sentences harmonious with his developed doctrine, the basic concept of justification still remains Augustinian. The change to full-fledged Lutheranism is probably first marked by *A Sermon on the Threefold Righteousness* published toward the end of the year 1518. In this sermon and in another which appeared not later than March 1519, Luther seems at last to have come out from under the wing of Augustine. He now speaks of Christ and his work from the manger to Calvary as constituting the righteousness of believers. This work of Christ blots out all sins in a moment, *omnia peccata in momento absorbens*. Here is an 'extrinsic justification', an 'alien righteousness', not something gradually built up within man but suddenly brought to him from outside. The *theologia crucis* is now not a cross-bearing by man in the steps of Christ; it is only the cross-bearing of Christ for the sinner. Relying wholly and singly on the work of Christ, enjoying all its effects here and now, the Christian (and this meant especially poor Luther himself!) can at once adopt a more confident attitude. He is no longer a wistful suppliant for a slow infusion of grace. He now has a joyful assurance of salvation, since Christ has already won the victory on his behalf. Now the secondary, slow process of sanctification—though this again springs solely from grace—can proceed. He is now already the child of God and by grace can be brought toward conformity with the divine will. A short passage in the second course of lectures on *Psalms*, also written late in 1518, seems in harmony with this same developed doctrine. The latter is again stated with great conviction and assurance in Luther's little book *Fourteen Consolations* written about August–September 1519 and sent in manuscript to Spalatin.

Hence we see Luther stress justifying faith from 1512, yet at first only in a limited Augustinian sense. But about the autumn of 1518 he breaks through to the 'extrinsic' conception ever since associated with his name. This cannot be found in Catholic doctrine, even among the so-called Reformers before the Reformation. It continues to be rejected even by those Catholic theologians most favourable to Luther's broad emphases on *sola gratia, sola fide*. From its emergence we may reasonably date the theological birth of Lutheran Protestantism, even though Luther's criticism of indulgences—a criticism which could well be formulated on merely Augustinian principles— had begun two years earlier. This dating fits satisfactorily with the hints left by Luther concerning his tower-experience, which we have taken to represent his achievement of the mature doctrine of imputation. He tells us, for example, that this experience occurred while he was working upon his second set of lectures on *Psalms*, and these we know he actually started to deliver at the beginning of 1519.

Whatever the importance of the tower-experience, it should not be regarded as a 'religious experience' as one applies this term either to medieval mystics or modern revivalists. It claimed to be a 'moment of truth' in a more literal and obvious sense. Luther was not concerned to achieve a revelation from within his own emotional resources. Long years earlier he had been 'converted', and acquired the marks of a deeply-felt personal religion. The tower-experience was something different; it taught him what he believed to be the true sense of the Scriptures, the understanding of something objective, of something God had long ago thrown open to the insight of men. To understand the Lutheran religion we have first to reckon with people who believed that the Bible, truly understood, contained all significant truth. While this commitment might cause them to quarrel with religious beliefs and practices sanctioned or connived at by the medieval Church, it nevertheless provided a safeguard against very different opponents: against those called in modern jargon the Spiritualists, the uncontrolled believers in the inner light who luxuriated in their subjective experiences and elevated them to the rank of divine revelation. Soon Luther and his followers would be challenged to demonstrate the difference between their own approach and that of these enthusiasts who exalted 'spirit' against 'book', who claimed that special insights were vouchsafed to pious weavers and tradesmen as well as to professors of biblical theology.

Chapter Three

Luther in Revolt, 1517-1520

ALONGSIDE the later stages of his theological development
Luther gradually came into conflict with the Church over
the question of indulgences. In March 1515 Leo X had author-
ised their use for the rebuilding of St. Peter's, and in Germany
the commissioners issued instructions which mentioned not only
the remission of the temporal penalties of sin, but also the 'full
remission of sins' to repentant purchasers. Though the Elector
Frederick excluded the indulgence-preachers from his lands,
his attitude was based not on religious principles but on his
determination to stop Saxon money leaving the country and to
protect the profits of his own shrines. Back in 1512 he had
actually agreed with Rome on the renewal of an indulgence to
raise money for building a bridge over the Elbe at Torgau,
while as late as 1518 he was still securing further privileges for
his relic-collection at Wittenberg. Even to Luther this ambivalent situation must have suggested a somewhat cautious
approach. When he first criticised indulgences in a sermon of
October 1516 at the Castle Church, he accepted the general
intentions of the Pope. In two sermons of 1517 his criticism
became blunter, stressing the great dangers of moral com-
placency and, while admitting the Pope's right to impose temporal penalties for sin, questioning whether the Pope's prayers
could really move God to pardon the penitents.

Meanwhile the matter developed a new dimension with the
special arrangements made between the Papacy, the banking-
house of Fugger at Augsburg, and Albert of Hohenzollern,
Archbishop of Magdeburg and administrator of the diocese of
Halberstadt. This worldly young man, still in his early twenties, wanted to add to his other opulent benefices the Archbishopric of Mainz, the holder of which was also senior

ecclesiastical Elector. The Pope demanded as his
less than 21,000 ducats, plus an additional 10,000 fo
ing him to hold all these offices together. To mee
sum, it was agreed that indulgences should be sold t
the lands of the Archbishopric of Mainz and those o. the dioceses of Magdeburg and Brandenburg. The Fuggers, having
advanced the money on Albert's behalf, were to reimburse
themselves from one half of the proceeds arising from the
indulgence and to forward the remaining half to Rome for the
rebuilding of St. Peter's.

Early in 1517 the Dominican Johann Tetzel, who had been
engaged on this type of work as early as 1502, was selling his
wares in the immediate neighbourhood of the Elector's territories. As he approached the little towns preceded by his cross
and the papal banner, he was received with flags, bells and
organ recitals. For the more critical observers the spectacle
was marred by the presence of the Fugger accountant, ever
recording and despatching the large sums collected from the
pious. Debarred by the Elector from Ernestine Saxony and by
his cousin Duke George from the Albertine lands, Tetzel nevertheless came so close that the Wittenbergers could easily cross
the border and purchase.

By the autumn and on his own bold initiative Luther decided
to stage a direct and general attack, and he posted up on
31 October his famous *Ninety-Five Theses* amid the annual fes-
tival when crowds of visitors came to Wittenberg to inspect the
Elector's relics. He soon sent copies of the *Theses* to Albert of
Hohenzollern, to the Bishop of Brandenburg and other nota-
bilites. They were probably printed in advance, and though no
copy of the first edition has survived, numerous others in both
German and Latin were pouring within a few weeks from the
presses at Leipzig, Madgeburg, Nuremberg and Basle. Already
Luther was making full use of the press for a direct appeal to
the German people. Read with due attention, the *Theses* seem
no mere list but a revelation of Luther's gifts as propagandist.
Though academic in outer form, they develop emotional over-
tones as they proceed. From number 42 to number 50 he re-
iterates incessantly and remorselessly the phrase *Docendi sunt*

christiani. But his aim is most deadly when he is calmest; he does not always use the bludgeon, and on occasion he can be a master of understatement:

50. Christians should be taught that if the Pope knew the exactions of the indulgence-preachers, he would rather the Church of St. Peter were reduced to ashes than be built with the skin, flesh and bones of his sheep.

. . . . .

81. This unbridled preaching of indulgences makes it difficult for learned men to guard the respect due to the Pope against false accusations, or at least from the keen criticisms of the laity;

82. They ask, e.g., Why does not the Pope liberate everyone from purgatory for the sake of love (a most holy thing) and because of the supreme necessity of their souls? This would be morally the best of all reasons. Meanwhile he redeems innumerable souls for money, a most perishable thing, with which to build St. Peter's Church, a very minor purpose.

. . . . .

86. Again, since the Pope's income today is larger than that of the wealthiest of wealthy men, why does he not build this one Church of St. Peter with his own money, rather than with the money of poor believers?

Along with a copy of the *Theses* Luther sent Archbishop Albert a letter in which forthright reproof was but faintly masked by expressions of personal humility. Here he quotes at second hand some near-blasphemous passages from Tetzel's preaching. Though these may have lost nothing in transit, other witnesses (and for that matter Tetzel's own sermon-notes) show the extent to which the incautious Dominican had played into Luther's hands.

Supposing the Elector Frederick to be encouraging his subject and anxious not to become the targets of German indignation, Albert and his supporters referred the matter to the

Pope. Leo X as yet sensed nothing more impo
squabble between German friars; he tried to sil
through the General of the Augustinian Order,
without effect to Luther's superior Staupitz. At this st ____ ____ner
was drawing closer to his old acquaintance the court-chaplain
Spalatin, and through him gaining the Elector's favour. Success
in this endeavour would soon become the crucial factor in his
exposed situation. Early in 1518 he published a *Sermon on Indulgence and Grace*, which went further than the *Theses*. Here
in blunt German he condemns indulgences as seeking to replace
the wholesome mental discomfort that penitent sinners should
be willing to undergo. "It is my wish and advice that nobody
should buy indulgences. Leave idle, sleepy Christians to buy
them and go your own way!" This popular pamphlet seems
to have circulated even more widely than the *Theses* themselves.

Under the protection of his prince, Luther visited Heidelberg
in April 1518 for the triennial convention of his Order. Here
he was well received and along with Staupitz entertained to
dinner by the brother of the Elector Palatine. In the convention Luther and his pupils defended his developing views on
justification by faith and aroused no more than the mildest
opposition. At this phase his immunity owed much to the
favourable attitude of the Augustinians, whose sympathy was
not a little enlarged by the fact that the rival Dominicans were
as yet his only bitter opponents. In general it may be supposed
that the rage of the latter added much to Luther's popularity,
for the Dominicans were most unpopular throughout German
society, lay and clerical alike. Yet strangely enough, he captured on this occasion a young Dominican who had been permitted to attend the Augustinian discussions and who was to
become one of the greatest of Protestant leaders. This was
Martin Bucer, who wrote a few days later to one of his
humanist friends in Basle, summarising Luther's contentions
and comparing his intelligence with that of St. Paul. "That
which Erasmus insinuates he speaks openly and freely." Opinion
now tended to go by age-groups and Luther's opinions were
soon to develop an immense appeal to critical young men of all

35

asses throughout Europe. On the other hand, when after this Heidelberg meeting Luther met his former Erfurt teachers von Usingen and Trutvetter, he found they no longer stood behind him. "I have great hope", he wrote to Spalatin, "that as Christ, when rejected by the Jews, went over to the Gentiles, so this true theology, rejected by opinionated old men, will pass over to the younger generation."

On his return Luther published a commentary on the *Theses* with a calculating but still polite letter of dedication to the Pope. But this commentary recalled the sins of Alexander VI and Julius II, and it demanded a general reform of the Church. While his case was still under consideration in Rome, he came under literary fire from the Dominican theologians of a rival northern university, that of Frankfurt-am-Oder, from Tetzel himself, and from a much more formidable opponent whose learning he greatly admired: Dr. Johann Eck, professor of theology at Ingolstadt. After Heidelberg it became obvious in Rome that the delinquent would never be silenced through his own Order, and under Dominican pressure the slow machinery of the Curia went into motion. At first, and ill-advisedly, Leo directed the Commissioner of the Sacred Palace, the Dominican Sylvester Prierias, to report on Luther's doctrines. Within three days, according to his own boast, Prierias wrote an attack on Luther as fluent in its humanist invective as it was exiguous in its theology. It did little save repeat the assertion of absolute papal authority accepted by the Lateran Council three years earlier. Luther received the document in August 1518 and, though somewhat shocked by this first direct condemnation from Rome, replied in more erudite but equally robust terms, making the satirical claim that he had penned his reply in only *two* days. In the same month he also received a summons demanding his presence within sixty days in Rome. Assuring the anxious Staupitz that these threats would not for a moment deflect him from his course, he appealed to his prince for protection. Frederick for his part did not wish to appear involved in Luther's actions and for this reason carefully refrained from associating with him in person. But despite his own profits from indulgences and relics, he showed from this point that he had no intention of surrendering his professor of theology to the tender mercies of Roman justice. Henceforth Luther's career became involved with the high politics and diplomacy of Europe: never again would it be wholly extricated from their slimy coils.

In July 1518 the Cardinal Thomas de Vio, called Cajetan, General of the Dominican Order, met the Imperial Diet at Augsburg. Though his main objective was to extract money for the Turkish campaign—and it is to the honour of the Roman Church that during Luther's career it seldom faltered in this task—he also attached great importance to silencing Luther, and he received encouragement when the Emperor Maximilian promised to execute the papal judgment against the friar. But the Emperor stood in no position to fulfil his promise, since he badly needed to placate the Elector Frederick, already the chief opponent of his scheme to ensure the election of his grandson Charles (who in 1516 had succeeded Ferdinand of Aragon as King of Spain) to the Imperial throne. The ambitious young King of France was already trying to bribe the German princes to ensure his own election, while for a time Frederick even debated the chances of a personal candidature, hoping he might attract any Electors who sought to compromise between Habsburg and Valois. In the event, Maximilian died the following January, and this prolonged crisis in the affairs of the Habsburg dynasty came at a most opportune moment for Luther. At Augsburg Cardinal Cajetan found himself forced to display great tact, since he found himself confronted by the daunting spectre of German anticlericalism.

In our allusions to Luther's background we have not hitherto done justice to the disapproval, jealousy and disgust felt by German laymen toward the clergy as a whole. In his *History of the Reformation in Germany* Leopold von Ranke discussed the popular literature of the two decades preceding Luther's revolt—Sebastian Brant, the *Fastnachtspiele*, the *Eulenspiegel*, the 1498 edition of *Reineke Fuchs*—and he concluded: "And if we enquire what characteristic they have in common, we find it to be that of hostility to the Church of Rome." If one sought parallel examples amid the governing classes in Germany, one

37

could find none more striking than the lists of *gravamina* directed at the Church by this and by several previous Diets of the Holy Roman Empire. Especially since the unprincipled misuse of German crusade-funds by Julius II, feeling had run high, and this 'official' criticism could hardly have been strengthened by Luther himself at his most vitriolic.

In addition to the explosive atmosphere of Germany, Leo and Cajetan had other motives for moderation in regard to Saxony and Luther. Both as a Medici and as a Pope, Leo had no desire to see the youthful Charles dominating Italy and Europe by his succession to the greatest agglomeration of lands and titles ever seen since the Carolingian age. Leo lacked prescience in religious affairs, yet the spectacle of a Papacy soon to be bullied and terribly endangered by the ambivalent Habsburgs leads one to credit him with a measure of political foresight. For the moment he was bound to play a double game. While calling publicly on the Elector to surrender Luther, he secretly encouraged Frederick's resistance to the Emperor's plans. In September he arranged to send a papal chamberlain, the young Saxon nobleman Karl von Miltitz, to call on Frederick with the much-coveted Golden Rose of Virtue, together with a new bundle of indulgences and privileges. At this time Luther had little inkling of the manner in which these eminent schemers were conspiring to preserve him. With little solidly assured support save that of his faculty at Wittenberg, he had the example of John Huss in mind as he left to appear before Cajetan at Augsburg. With a touch of humour he recalls his thoughts in the *Table Talk*: "I clearly saw my grave ready and kept repeating to myself, 'What a disgrace I shall be to my dear parents'." Yet in a contemporary letter to a fellow-Augustinian he speaks in far more exalted terms of the perennial necessity to uphold the word of Christ, even amid the hourly prospect of death. "It was bought with death; it has spread with many a death; with manifold death must it be preserved or restored." While matters did not so develop, the clash with Cajetan at least marked the definitive parting of Luther's ways from those of Rome; it was among the severest

38

of the many tests to which his immense obstinacy was ever subjected.

Luther went to Augsburg with expenses paid by the Elector and accompanied by experienced councillors from the Saxon court. At the hearings on 12–14 October 1518 Cajetan and his fellow Italians must have sensed in the background the pressures of German opinion: in the absence of Maximilian and of the German prelates they enjoyed little local support. As an upright critic of abuses Cajetan was personally respected by Luther, even though he was shortly to become the target of bitter attacks by Ulrich von Hutten and other German humanists. Confronted by Luther for three days, this eminent Dominican strove to maintain a fatherly attitude, but there occurred some loud outbursts on both sides. He began by demanding that Luther should recant two errors: his denial that indulgences were founded on the merits of Christ and the saints, and his suggestion that the efficacy of the sacrament depended upon the faith of the communicant. The discussion later moved to the problems concerning papal authority over the Church and over the Scriptures, but since Cajetan appealed to papal bulls and Thomist philosophy, Luther to his own interpretation of the Bible, no true dialogue could ensue. Finally, on the advice of the Saxon councillors, who apparently heard of some plot to arrest Luther or offer him violence, he fled on the night of 20 October from Augsburg to Nuremburg. In that famous city, the heart of the German Renaissance, he met the humanist patrician Willibald Pirckheimer and numerous other influential backers.

On Martin's return to Wittenberg there followed anxious days when some of his friends feared the Elector would abandon him. But in December the discreet old politician came into the open with a reply to Cajetan, affirming that no one had yet proved heresy against Luther. The latter then proceeded to put forth in print—but without Frederick's approval—his account of the exchanges at Augsburg. Here he compared his situation to that of the great hebraist Reuchlin, at this time also a victim of Dominican persecution. He also argued that Cajetan confronted him with a novel claim: that the Pope stands superior

39

to Councils, Scriptures and the whole Church. Luther now questioned the supremacy of the Roman Church over all others and denied that the merits of Christ are at the Pope's disposal. Soon after his return he formally appealed to a General Council, and he again publicised his action by publishing and circulating the appeal on a large scale. Here he entered another mine-field of controversy. The impetus of the Conciliar Movement was not yet spent, and even in the previous year the university of Paris had appealed to a future General Council against the decisions of the papally-controlled Council recently held at the Lateran.

During these manoeuvres the papal nuncio Miltitz had started for Saxony, and as he crossed southern Germany he noted much evidence of public support for the rebel. Meeting Luther at last in January 1519, he spoke as Saxon to Saxon and convinced his often susceptible hearer of the intense anxiety occasioned in Rome: he even induced Luther to draft a humble and conciliatory letter to the Pope. This was never in fact despatched, for though the contact with Miltitz ended in protestations of friendship, Luther soon hardened again. He sensed both the unchanging attitude of Leo, and the insidious pressures brought against himself by Miltitz in private interviews with the Elector. His studies were also convincing him that the Papacy, while potentially valuable as an organiser of the temporal affairs of the Church, had no basis in the law of God and no divinely-conferred spiritual jurisdiction.

At this juncture the Emperor Maximilian died, and Leo renewed his efforts through Miltitz to prevent the election of young King Charles to the Imperial throne. But the Elector Frederick now showed himself proof against French money, papal diplomacy and personal ambition alike. In June at Frankfurt-am-Main he realised that the preponderant weight of German opinion still favoured the Habsburg candidate, and he ensured the election of Charles. Showing great caution, he continued to deal with Luther indirectly through Spalatin. Meanwhile his cousin Duke George of Albertine Saxony wanted church reforms but rejected Luther's doctrines and soon became the Reformer's inveterate enemy. Another pertinacious adversary was Dr. Johann Eck, who now induced Duke George and the university of Leipzig to allow a disputation between Luther and himself. This clash between established Leipzig and red-brick Wittenberg also reflected the rivalry between the two Saxon states. But at this time George furthered the plan out of genuine sportsmanship. When counselled not to admit Luther, he retorted, "What good is a soldier if he is not permitted to fight, a sheep-dog if he may not bark, a theologian if he may not debate?"

Despite a coarse countenance, a stentorian voice and an ample fund of vanity, Eck was a highly professional disputant armed with outstanding erudition, memory and agility of mind. He also believed in his religious cause and remained a staunch, tireless champion of Catholicism in a period when Catholicism had strangely few defenders of such calibre. However orthodox, Eck was no obscurantist but well versed in humanist scholarship and far from unmindful of abuses, even those of the indulgence-system. The breadth of his interests and his rational approach are expressed in a number of works which, after centuries of Protestant abuse, have received due praise in our own day. For his part Luther studied hard in preparation for an encounter more intellectually formidable than those he had hitherto faced. He worked especially upon the papal decretals in order to be able to prove that the papal supremacy had grown up only during the last four centuries.

On the Leipzig adventure he was accompanied by two Wittenberg colleagues whose careers were to be variously and dramatically interwoven with his own. Much the elder of these was Andreas Bodenstein, usually known from his Franconian birthplace as Carlstadt. After study at Erfurt and Cologne this rather bizarre academic had come in 1505 to Wittenberg, where he had published a defence of Thomist philosophy and become dean of the arts faculty. For some years he turned to theology, but in 1515–16 he visited Rome to study law and picked up an easily-won doctorate from the university of Siena. About this time a newly-found devotion to St. Augustine brought him round to views similar to those of Luther, who cannot yet have sensed the contentious and unreliable temperament accompanying Carlstadt's very real courage and ability. Carlstadt had recently been in literary conflict with Eck, who had attacked Luther through him and who was now hoping to pay off the scores against both the Wittenbergers. Luther's second companion was Philip Melanchthon, whose career, beginning as that of a teenage prodigy, had just brought him at the age of twenty-one to the chair of Greek in Wittenberg. Lacking Luther's intensity of experience and hard-won convictions, Philip nevertheless soon became the beloved and the leading disciple. Luther imaginatively pictured St. Paul himself as a 'poor, thin little man, like Magister Philippus'. Within two or three years the latter was displaying to the full that gift of cool, orderly statement which proved the perfect complement to Luther's volcanic utterance. A pious scholar yet no religious genius, he ended by making a contribution to Lutheranism as ambivalent as it was weighty. Soon after his arrival in Wittenberg he began that course of lectures on *Romans* which formed the nucleus of his *Loci Communes*, the standard compendium of Lutheran theology. At length published late in 1521, this latter went through 17 editions during the subsequent two years and was hailed by Luther himself as 'worthy not only of immortality, but of a place in the canon of Scripture'. He would have been less enthusiastic had he foreseen the final outcome of those strange metamorphoses which the *Loci* underwent in later editions.

The Leipzig disputation, preceded by music, formal oratory and a dinner, was conducted according to elaborate rules before neutral umpires. Despite its faintly ludicrous atmosphere it testifies to the touching belief of the age in academic debate. Few episodes in Luther's life have been documented from so many angles. The dispute between Eck and Carlstadt on the problem of free will saw Eck winning the applause, even though there may now appear some obvious weaknesses in his position. When Luther faced Eck on the issue of papal authority, spectators who had not yet seen the former were impressed both by the originality of his ideas and by his personal characteristics: the austere, emaciated frame, the clear, pleasing voice, the strange and striking eyes—demonic eyes, according to Catholic observers. He gave an impression of geniality, except at the moments when he was roused to passion. Throughout their long debates, Eck continually charged Luther with repeating the heresies of Huss and the Bohemians, a popular line in a German frontier-city. At first Luther violently denied any debt to Huss and sought to extricate himself from seeming to attack the Council of Constance, which had condemned the Bohemian heretic. Yet in due course he admitted that among the Hussite articles 'there are many that are plainly very Christian and evangelical, which the Universal Church cannot condemn'. On the morrow of the conference he in fact received congratulations from certain Bohemian divines. While the evidence contradicts any notion that Hussitism stirred him to revolt, it is true that from this stage he came to appreciate its congenial features.

The exhausting disputations ended on 15 July 1519, after a further clash between Eck and Carlstadt on the topic of grace and free will. On this last day some of the Leipzig doctors fell asleep and had to be roused for dinner. Both parties retired amid mutual complaints about foul play in the debating-chamber and threats of violence made elsewhere by partisans. The Wittenbergers went home, denouncing Eck's bluster and the obvious favouritism shown by Duke George's court. Eck stayed on at Leipzig for eleven days, proclaiming his own triumph and receiving lavish hospitality. But much to his and the Duke's annoyance the umpires from Erfurt and Paris refused on technical grounds to award victory to either side.

There followed an involved pamphlet-war by many champions on both sides, and in its course Luther clarified some of the points he would make in the famous tractates of the following year. He denied, for example, that either the canon law or the practice of secret confession have any divine sanction. Mere abuse also had its part. Luther upbraided Eck with the stinging charge that he made even Prierias look like a man of learning. Eck's even ruder reply called Luther a pseudo-prophet and a filthy monk, while nevertheless conceding that after a course of two years tuition under Eck he might be turned into a tolerable theologian. Luther then spoke of Eck's 'foul and filthy epistle', charging him with the Pelagian heresy. Willibald

Pirckheimer of Nuremberg intervened with *The Purified Eck*, a rather revolting satire describing the removal of Eck's errors and vices by means of a surgical operation. These exchanges recall the rugged methods of the *Epistolae Obscurorum Virorum*, which a few years earlier had excoriated the Cologne Dominicans. Luther himself had not much use for frivolous satire, but amid the blows and counter-blows of 1519 he found time to attack Jakob von Hochstraten, the Dominican who had taken the lead against Reuchlin and in a gross spirit of obscurantism had destroyed the Talmudic Books.

In 1518–19 signs of enthusiasm for Luther multiply in the records of the humanist circles, which saw in his opponents the same spirit they were denouncing in those of Reuchlin. The surviving correspondence, no doubt a tithe of that originally written along these lines, also includes many letters of support from divines soon to be prominent in the coming religious battle throughout Europe: from Wolfgang Capito and Martin Bucer, then respectively in Basle and Heidelberg, from Justus Jonas, at the time rector of Erfurt University. On the other hand, even at this early date a split between Luther and Erasmus can be observed. Already in March 1517 Luther's former admiration was yielding to the conviction that the religion of Erasmus concerned itself insufficiently with Christ and with grace. In 1518 Luther regretted the Erasmian practice of laughing at evil in the Church when one should be lamenting it with groans. He nevertheless eagerly read the works of Erasmus as he succeeded in acquiring copies, and however deep he felt the chasm between the Christian moralism of Erasmus and his own religion of justifying faith, he was bound to admire Erasmus as the major advocate of reform. In March 1519 he wrote directly to the great man, asking for his support, and in reply received a friendly letter urging peaceable moderation. While favouring Luther's attack on abuses, Erasmus feared the assiduous attempts of Hochstraten and other reactionary enemies to depict him as a heretical supporter of Luther, and he long maintained the pose that he never read Luther's books.

When in 1521 Luther appeared before the enthroned powers at the Diet of Worms he was anything but an 'obscure monk'.

That he already stood among the celebrities of the age is clear enough from the sources of the previous two years. "All Switzerland, Constance, Augsburg and a large part of Italy hang upon Luther," wrote the Freiburg jurist Zasius in December 1519. His astonishing range of sermons and tracts both devotional and polemical had anticipated nearly all the ideas to be given classic expression in the more famous writings of the year 1520. A collected volume of his Latin works had been published by Froben at Basle in October 1518. He was now acting as spiritual counsellor to many German clerics and laymen. While Rome, Cologne and Leipzig saw a ferment of activity by his opponents, supporters were writing to him from all parts of the German-speaking world, as well as from Paris and other foreign cities. Stories even circulated to the effect that he was the offspring of a demon succubus, born in Bohemia, and he felt constrained to put the record straight by addressing a memoir to Spalatin describing his more respectable family-background.

Luther's literary *annus mirabilis* 1520 saw the appearance of about 24 publications. Of these, some half-dozen demand close attention both on account of their phenomenal impact on German society and as expressions, at once perfected and popularised, of his mature thought. While our present purpose requires some attempt to describe their content, we are bound to stress the fact that only the original texts or good and full translations can do justice to Luther the writer, and hence begin to explain his enormous following.

The *Sermon on Good Works* (published in May) takes the form of an analysis of the Ten Commandments; it is a brief compendium of practical theology for the unlearned. Good works include all the duties and actions of everyday living, insofar as they are inspired and informed by faith. Faith resembles physical health: as all the limbs of a healthy body are equally healthy, so good works do not among themselves vary in quality. They are mere limbs appended to the single body of faith. The poor man who clings to faith in adversity does more good than all those who found churches or run around on long pilgrimages. The writer's protest against formalism then prompts him to attack both the trafficking in alleged spiritual gifts, which he ascribes to Roman religion, and the decay of moral and social life in Germany itself. With his dream of a patriarchal and rural society, he condemns the German excesses in eating, drinking and apparel, the charging of interest, which 'everywhere destroys land, people and cities', the disorder and discontent among the artisans, the injustices perpetrated by the governing classes. He had no sympathy with the social-economic features of an age marked by inflation, banking, enclosure by landlords and radical proletarian movements. These he reviewed in moral and religious terms based not merely on a mythical golden age when all men knew their duty, but upon his sense of the helplessness of human nature uninspired by faith. He bade men throw off their chains not by forcible action but by entry into a world of the spirit, a world unassailable by ill fortune and by the temptations which beset all mortal life.

Also in April 1520 Luther had published his *Sermon on the Mass*. For him the service is 'not a work but an exercise in faith alone'. It has been distorted from apostolic simplicity by rich vestments, pompous prayers of human invention, above all by conceiving the mass to be a repetition of Christ's unrepeatable sacrifice on the Cross. Luther then proceeds naturally to another of his basic teachings: that the Christian minister differs from the layman only in respect of certain religious duties or functions he must perform. He does not belong to a separate order of men marked with indelible characteristics. Faith is the true office of a priest; therefore all Christians are priests, men and women, old and young, master and servant, mistress and maid, scholar and layman. As for the administration of communion in both kinds, the chief demand of the Hussites, this he does not regard as a matter of first importance, yet he denies the Pope any right to withhold the cup from the laity, since the Pope has not the slightest power to exceed the commands of Christ.

In June Luther pursued this theme further with a tract *On the Papacy at Rome*. Ostensibly directed against his Leipzig opponents, it was in effect a sweeping denunciation of the claim that Christendom lay under a divinely-appointed Roman monarchy. The Russians, Greeks and Bohemians, having the same faith and baptism as we Germans, are not made heretics simply because they do not pay to have their bishops confirmed by Rome. The kingdom of God is within us, and Christendom is composed of the souls of the faithful; it is not an ecclesiastical version of an earthly empire. Christ is the true High Priest, while the Pope is 'the real Anti-Christ of whom all the Scripture speaks'. This inflammatory manifesto ran through at least a dozen editions.

Three succeeding works are deservedly regarded as classics of the Lutheran Reformation, though in fact most of their leading ideas can be found earlier. They differ strikingly from each other and together demonstrate Luther's immense range. They are nevertheless complementary and all singularly applicable to the current situation.

To the Christian Nobility of the German Nation (August 1520) is a natural favourite with secular historians, for it covers the whole gamut of the nation's social and ecclesiastical problems. It is indeed one of the great reform-programmes of western literature, appealing over the heads of the churchmen to the nationalism, the utilitarianism and the anticlericalism of the lay governing class. Our German rulers, long fooled by the greedy cormorants of Rome, should cease paying annates or taking their legal cases up to the Curia. Secular rulers everywhere should agree to establish national churches. Christian people are all priests, though called to fill different offices. Vows of celibacy should be abolished, monks allowed to leave their cloisters, religious houses be converted into schools, pilgrimages abolished, rites and ceremonies simplified, the Hussite heresy re-examined in a more sympathetic spirit. Luther condemns the betrayal of the safeconduct given to Huss and has some things to say of heresy which were soon to be echoed round Europe by radical sectarians as well as by followers of Luther:

Heretics ought to be persuaded by argument, and not by fire; and this was the way of the early Fathers. If it were wise policy to suppress heretics by burning them, then the executioners would be the most learned teachers on earth. We

47

should have no need to study books any longer, for he who could overthrow his fellow by violence would have the right to burn him at the stake.

Luther then turns to the universities, which he regards as in urgent need of reform. The study of canon law ought to be discontinued: languages, mathematics and history made to replace Aristotelian logic and philosophy. The textual study of the Bible needs freeing from the dominance of outworn textbooks. In every town there should be a school for girls as well as one for boys, and the Gospel as taught by Christ should be the central feature of the curriculum. While his tract is addressed to the laity, Luther does not hesitate to attack lay gluttony, luxury and ostentation. Hoping to recover a golden age by the rehabilitation of agriculture, he calls on the rulers to bridle the rapacious financiers, mentioning the Fuggers by name. Mindful of the evils of poverty and begging, he calls for the establishment of a parish poor-law system. In short, alongside the strong prejudices and the impracticable proposals, no more concentrated dose of common sense was ever administered to a corrupt and hypocritical society. For us it is marred, like so much of Luther's writing, by that simplification, that growing monomania which caused him to trace so great a part of the human predicament to Rome. On the other hand, the specific criticisms and positive proposals of the treatise reveal a high idealism, a social morality independent alike of ancient vested interests and of current trends in a swiftly-changing world.

By way of contrast with this vernacular work addressed to laymen, *The Babylonian Captivity of the Church* (October 1520) is in Latin; the author knows it to be strong meat for the laity and addresses himself mainly to the priesthood. To his displeasure it was translated and published the following year by his enemy Thomas Murner. *The Babylonian Captivity* is a treatise on the sacraments, and more broadly speaking, a plea for the abolition of non-biblical theology and of man-made ecclesiastical laws. The sacraments Luther would reduce to three: the eucharist, baptism and confession. Later he was to subtract the last-named, leaving only the two plainly attested by Scripture. He is convinced that Christ meant all men to

48

communicate in both kinds. In denying the cup to the laity, the Roman Church is heretical; the Bohemians and the Greeks, who allow it, are orthodox because they adhere to the plain meaning of the Gospels. Again, even in the consecrated elements the bread and wine are still substantially present; they have not become mere 'accidents' as taught by the Thomists and the Aristotelian dogma of Rome. For twelve hundred years the right belief prevailed until Aristotelian philosophy began to run away with Christian truth. The Aristotelians who teach transubstantiation, and not Wycliffe who denied it, deserve the charge of heresy. Luther then introduces his own eucharistic teaching, later to be known under the misleading title of consubstantiation.

> Why could not Christ maintain his body within the substance of bread as truly as within its accidents? Iron and fire are two substances which mingle together in red-hot iron in such a way that every part contains both iron and fire. Why cannot the glorified body of Christ be similarly found in every part of the substance of the bread?

This doctrine he elaborated in 1528 in his *Confession concerning the Lord's Supper.* The notion of a Real Presence he made an absolute dogma, even as he rejected transubstantiation. He could not accept the words *hoc est corpus meum* in a merely figurative sense. Fallen man needs a sensible vehicle for communion with God, and since the person of Christ is indivisible, he is present at the eucharist not only in his divine but in his human nature. On the other hand, *The Babylonian Captivity* repeats that the mass is neither a saving 'good work' nor a repetition of Christ's sacrifice. It should be stripped of elaborate vestments, incense, long prayers and other late accretions. It is a covenant or promise, also a memorial service. We go to it trusting only in faith, not in confession or in any other processes of self-preparation. The benefits of a mass cannot be transferred to someone else, any more than can baptism, or penance, or final unction. And why may it be celebrated in Greek or Latin and not also in German, or any other language? Likewise with baptism: it is not the act itself but the sacramental faith which justifies. And in a remarkably imaginative passage on baptism, Luther sees this sacrament not merely as a cleansing from sin but also as a symbol of the justification and salvation of man, as a dying to an old way of life and a resurrection to the new way, produced by faith.

Hereabouts Luther has some burning sentences on ecclesiasticism and liberty:

> The Church is smothered by endless regulations about rites and ceremonies . . . faith in Christ is obstructed. Therefore I declare that neither pope nor bishop nor any other person has the right to impose a syllable of law upon a Christian man without his own consent . . . the churchmen of today are most energetic guardians of ecclesiastical liberty, in the sense of the liberty to use and possess the stones, timber, lands and rents. 'Ecclesiastical' has come to mean the same as 'spiritual'. By this same false terminology they not only put the true liberty of the Church in bonds, but utterly destroy it.

Again he appeals for spiritual liberty in strains which not even his own later and more timid retractions could silence.

> It is solely on behalf of this liberty that I cry aloud; and I do so with a good conscience, and in the faith that it is impossible for either men or angels rightfully to impose even a single law upon Christians except with their own consent, for we are free from all things. Yet whatever the impositions may be, they should be borne in such a manner that we preserve liberty of conscience, the conscience that knows and affirms unhesitatingly that an injury is being done to it, even while it glories in bearing that injury.

The electrifying effect of these phrases can not only be imagined but proved. Yet even in these early days Luther did not aim to grant free private judgment or freedom of worship to extremists or enthusiasts; he aimed in fact to liberate the conscience from ecclesiastical rules in order to bind it all the more tightly to the Scriptures, to what he considered clear and objective biblical precepts. His optimism was soon to receive some rude shocks at the hands of the radicals. Even in the

50

Babylonian Captivity he is already concerned to qualify another of his dramatic expressions. He does not mean by 'the priest-hood of all believers' that the Church can manage without an appointed ministry, yet he envisages the latter as a preaching pastorate. "Those men who are ordained merely to read the canonical hours may be papal priests, but they are not Christian priests."

The final work in this famous group, *The Freedom of a Christian* (November 1520), was at first written in Latin with the intention that it should be sent to the Pope, but Luther immediately produced a free translation for the German public. In tone and purpose it could hardly differ more widely from those of the foregoing treatises; it is devotional and non-pole-mical. Admirably written, it is in every sense a Christian classic, and in reading it one comes to appreciate that somewhat absurd title applied by admirers to Luther: the Swan of Wittenberg. The title of the treatise represents only one half of Luther's paradox based upon the paradoxical passages in the thought of St. Paul:

A Christian is free and independent in every respect, a bond-servant to none.
A Christian is a dutiful servant in every respect, owing a duty to everybody.

A man's soul is regenerated by the Gospel message, is restored to freedom by grace through faith; yet insofar as he remains a creature of flesh in a human society, the man is chained by law and discipline. Christian liberty is free, joyful, creative, even though expressed in loving obedience to God and service to other men. What makes a man acceptable in God's eyes? Not ecclesiastical observances, but the fact that God has accom-plished the unmerited miracle of grace in his heart. This miracle will occur in God's time only; a man can do little save accept it in humility, in trust, in the desire to use the gift only as God wills. Here Luther's metaphors are characteristically bold and striking:

Is that not a happy household, when Christ, the rich, noble and virtuous bridegroom takes the poor, despised wicked little harlot in marriage, sets her free from all evil, and decks her with all good things? If a man were so foolish as to think that by good works he would become godly, free, blessed or a Christian, he would lose both faith and all else. He would be like the dog which, while carrying a piece of meat in its mouth, snapped at its reflection in the water, and thereby lost the meat and spoiled the reflection.

He frankly faces the charge of antinomianism, one already common and destined to be repeated on countless future occasions:

Oh then, if faith is the whole thing and sufficient in itself to make one religious, why are good works required? We shall be in a good situation without doing anything at all! No my dear fellow, it is not so at all . . . . Good works proceed logically from a godly and good person, ... just as faith makes one godly, so also does it produce good works.

And these principles he hammers home by a series of effective analogies:

When a consecrated bishop consecrates churches, confirms, or discharges other duties of his office, these duties do not make him a bishop. Were he not already consecrated a bishop, these same duties would be foolish and in vain. In the same way a Christian who is consecrated by faith, and who also does good, is not made a better or more consecrated Christian by his works, for only an increase of faith effects this . . . . good and devout works never make a man good and dutiful, but a good and religious man does good and religious works.

Intentions and objectives are the test of beneficence:

But I counsel you, if you want to pray, fast, or make an endowment, let it not be with the idea that you will benefit yourself. Rather do it freely in order that others may benefit; do it for their advantage—then you will be a real Christian.

When we have acknowledged the verve and the freshness of

this little work, we may well agree that it is not one of its author's most precise pieces of thinking. Yet the common man, who did not sense the depths below these limpid surfaces, could hardly remain in doubt as to the general purport of Luther's message and the breadth of the gap between it and the pious fiscality of the time. One need not be a Protestant to reflect how desperately something of the sort needed saying in that calculating period of bankers' Christianity, when for long years the financier family of Medici directed fund-raising from the papal throne itself, and the Fuggers sought with no little success to manage both Papacy and Empire.

By the end of 1520 Luther had not merely excogitated his message but had delivered it with the utmost pungency and force to the German nation. Moreover, he had issued a clear directive to practical and public action in Church and State. His influence was beginning to be felt even beyond the German-speaking areas of Europe. Meanwhile in Rome and elsewhere his opponents, headed by the indomitable Eck, strained every nerve to prevent him from disrupting Christendom, an outcome they foresaw more clearly than he. On 15 June 1520 was issued the Bull *Exsurge Domine*: "Let the Lord arise and his enemies be scattered." Without theological argument it lists 41 beliefs attributed to Luther and orders the books containing them to be burned. Doubtless following some marginal differences of opinion in the Curia, it avoids saying precisely which of these beliefs are heretical, as distinct from merely offensive or scandalous. Luther's attacks on purgatory, on the penitential system, on indulgences, on papal authority itself, naturally bulk large. His views on the eucharist receive little attention, apart from his insistence upon communion in both kinds for the laity. While his dislike of monastic views and his assertions regarding the priesthood of all believers are ignored, he is duly condemned for stressing the impotence and sinfulness of all human effort. Somewhat oddly, space is found to charge him with declaring that the burning of heretics is against the will of the Spirit, and that the warfare against the Turks is resistance to a divine visitation. Finally, Luther and his supporters are warned to renounce their errors and burn their writings within sixty days. If he does not recant or appear personally in Rome, he and they are notorious and obstinate heretics, whom both the spiritual and the temporal authorities are obliged to arrest and deliver to Rome.

This document reached Luther through the rector of his university on 11 October, the day of his final interview with Miltitz. As usual, he merely hardened under attack and delivered the counter-punch. In the November he produced *Against the Accursed Bull of Antichrist*, a sharp and sarcastic appeal to the common people, pretending that the Bull must be a falsification by his enemy Eck. Meantime Luther's books were burned at the Catholic centres of Louvain and Cologne, both visited for the ceremony by the legate Jerome Aleander. At Mainz a similar gesture was held up by popular resentment duly stimulated by the humanists, who continued to see the attack on Luther in terms of clerical obscurantism. Finally on 10 December the Wittenberg faculty and the whole body of students gathered outside the Elster Gate of the town to hold a rival ceremony. A fire being lit, Luther placed upon it a copy of the Bull, adding for good measure copies of the canon law and other monuments of papalism. This flamboyant gesture had become necessary to Luther's purpose in an age deeply impressed by pantomime. More important still, he immediately exploited the act by publishing an *apologia*, which reached at least ten impressions by the end of the month. For some time he had realised there could be no turning back; he was now extremely concerned that the world should know it too.

Chapter Four

Luther and the Nation, 1521–1525

THE despatches sent to Rome by the papal nuncio Aleander provide a vivid picture of the German situation at the end of 1520, when the youthful Emperor began to press Elector Frederick to bring Luther before the forthcoming Diet at Worms. Despite this action, Aleander distrusted the Imperial ministers Chièvres and Gattinara, whom he alleged to be conciliating German opinion; this process they would follow up, he imagined, by a great march of German armies to Rome for the crowning of Charles and the assertion of his sovereignty over southern Italy. The German princes and bishops needed careful nursing; even Archbishop Albert of Mainz, influenced by the Elector Frederick, had anti-Roman advisers. Frederick himself lay under the direct influence of Luther's enthusiastic followers. The lesser people were all ranged against Aleander: the lawyers, the humanists, the knights and poorer nobility, even many of the monks and friars, both inside and outside Luther's own Order. The common people were supporting Luther without really understanding his doctrine, their main motive being a blind hatred of Rome. They were buying pictures of Luther decorated as a saint, his head surmounted by a dove and a halo. From Franz von Sickingen's castle of Ebernburg, a day's journey from Worms, the notorious pamphleteer Ulrich von Hutten was pouring forth torrential attacks on Aleander, while other hostile knights were ready to ambush him if he left Worms.

Ample evidence suggests this was by no means a purely alarmist report, and Aleander did right to stress the popular enthusiasm behind Luther and the threatening demeanour of the knights. At the beginning of the year Hutten had offered Luther his protection and that of his powerful friend Sickingen; in June Sylvester von Schaumberg, hearing that the Reformer might be forced to flee to the Bohemians, offered him a body-guard of a hundred knights. This impoverished, discontented, lawless, yet still formidable class wanted above all to smash the prince-bishops, the jurists and the bankers; in two years' time it would make a final, ferocious bid to dominate the Empire.

On the eve of Worms Luther was writing in German an attack on the papal Bull and engaging in an abusive pamphlet-battle with his enemy Hieronymus Emser of Leipzig. He also expressed his eagerness to attend the Diet and knew he would not stand there alone. He received visits from the Elector of Brandenburg and the Duke of Pomerania on their way to Worms, and he heard that Christian II of Denmark had pre-vented the university of Copenhagen from condemning his works. And even though he doubtless realised the dubious quality of their emotions, the vociferous support of the Fran-conian knights and humanists must have afforded him no little encouragement.

In January 1521 the members of the Diet and their thousands of followers poured in and wrangled furiously over the limited accommodation at Worms. The case of Martin Luther was not the dominant item on the agenda, which concerned the political rather than the religious cohesion of the Empire. Toward this objective the new Emperor had all too little to contribute. He spoke no word of German and was under the sway of his Netherlandish advisers. Threatened by revolt in Spain, his revenue both from that source and from others remained quite inadequate to his immense responsibilities. One of Sickingen's anticlerical followers, threatening to descend upon Worms and 'carve up' the prelates and priests, remarked that the task would be simple, since the Emperor did not have 'four cripples' to defend himself and keep order.

Charles had indeed little behind him save his great patronage in Church and Empire, together with the old magic of the Imperial crown, recently though not very usefully intensified by the romantic flourishes of the humanists and of the late Emperor Maximilian. The Habsburg jaw, the severe adenoids, the formal, reserved manner, all these helped to deprive Charles of personal magnetism. As yet he had given little public evidence of that cautious resolution, that high sense of duty which distinguished him in later years. His piety was firm but conventional; he had not yet acquired the critical independence of spirit which might conceivably have enabled him to take over Luther's national movement. At this early stage, when there was still room for manoeuvre, a cleverer Emperor might at least have manipulated the antipapal revolt of the Germans as a weapon to extract sweeping reforms from the Papacy. But amid such strictures one should never lose sight of the fact that Charles was also the Catholic King of Catholic Spain.

When the Diet met in January 1521 Aleander besought the papal Chancellor not to allow any further inflaming of German opinion. Nine tenths of the people, he averred, were shouting "Luther!" and the other tenth "Death to the Court of Rome!". In Worms itself the presses were issuing Lutheran works under his nose and that of the Emperor. To get his own work done, Aleander had to offer heavy bribes to the local printers. Even the passers-by cursed him and toyed with their swords. He dared not publish a new bull against the heretics. This situation in Aleander's view owed much to the work of Erasmus in stirring up German anticlericalism; many people, he remarks, even thought Erasmus the real author of some of the books ostensibly by Luther. As expected, the early stages of the Diet itself were marked by strong attacks on Roman abuses and by a general disinclination to condemn Luther unheard, as Aleander requested. The Emperor himself adopted a mild attitude, in part motivated by current plans for a marriage between his sister and the nephew of Elector Frederick. Faced by the ever-present menace of France and gradually deserted by the Swiss, who had been offered better military contracts by the French, Charles could in any event hardly afford to quarrel with his German subjects. In March he issued an edict condemning Luther's heresies and forbidding their dissemination in print, but it took little effect and in Nuremberg the placards were torn down. When, on the other hand, Charles at last agreed to give Luther a safeconduct to attend the Diet, people could not help recalling how the Council of Constance had violated a former Emperor's safeconduct and burned John Huss.

On 2 April Luther's little party left Wittenberg, well provided with funds by electoral officials and by the university. The city of Wittenberg supplied a wagon and three horses. Even the unfriendly Duke George gave a permit to enable them to cross his lands, while his city councillors at Leipzig assembled to honour them with wine on their arrival two days later. The group included the theologian Nicholas Amsdorf and at Erfurt it was joined by Luther's other close associate, Justus Jonas. Here the celebrated Latinist Helius Eobanus Hessus produced four elegies in Luther's honour, while a great congregation assembled to hear him preach in the Augustinian chapel. The frail portico of the latter began to crack, but Luther averted a panic by calming the crowd and dismissing the event as a typical ruse of the devil. From this point the rest of his progress was marked by a popular acclaim worth as much as an official safeconduct. He reached Worms on 16 April, and the momentous events of the next ten days were to be watched and recorded in much detail by friends and foes alike. On 17 April Luther was summoned before the Emperor and all the great men of Germany in the smaller hall of the bishop's palace, packed on his arrival to suffocation. Confronted by a list of his books, he was asked whether he was responsible for writing them, whether he stood by the opinions advanced therein or wished to revoke any. In a low voice, nervously as his critics thought, he acknowledged his authorship and requested time for deliberation on the second point. Charles was unimpressed by his appearance and is said to have remarked, "This man will never make me a heretic."

The following afternoon the session was transferred to the larger hall of the palace, but here also the press became so great that even the Emperor had difficulty in reaching his seat. Luther had now recovered his normal confidence and while awaiting his ordeal in the courtyard he jovially greeted an acquaintance with enquiries about the man's family. Luther himself later recalled that, once inside, he was sweating profusely as he began his carefully prepared statement. He distinguished three elements in his writings. The parts dealing with faith and morals needed no revocation, for they had been accepted as useful even by his enemies. Those attacking the papacy and its claims could not be revoked without exposing the poor German people to continued oppression. "Then, good God, I should be an instrument for evil and tyranny!" The third group of writings, directed against the defenders of the Roman tyranny, might have gone further in violence than befitted his position, yet still he could not substantially revoke them. "For I do not set myself up to be a saint, nor do I argue about my own life, but about the doctrines of Christ." Even so, he was willing to hear charges against his works, and if he could be convinced of error by reference to the Prophets and Evangelists, he would be the first to throw his books into the flames.

The inquisitor and jurist von Eck (not to be confused with the famous theologian) then charged Luther with making the responses conventional to heretics ever since the time of the Arians, in fact with repeating the errors of the Waldensians, of Wycliffe and Huss. Von Eck demanded a clear and unambiguous answer. Would he recant or not? The crisis had arrived. Luther's reply was brief and to the point:

Unless I am convinced by the testimony of Scripture or by evident reasoning—for I trust neither in Popes nor in Councils alone, since it is obvious that they have often erred and contradicted themselves—unless I am convinced by Scripture, which I have mentioned, and unless my conscience is made captive by God's Word, I cannot and will not recant, since it is hard, unprofitable and dangerous to act against one's conscience.

And then he broke into his mother-tongue, *Gott helf mir, Amen*! The oft-repeated story that he also added *Ich kann nicht anders . . . . hier stehe ich* represents an uncertain and much later Wittenberg tradition, unsupported by the contemporary accounts.

As Luther was dismissed and made his way down the seething streets, a rumour broke out that he was to be arrested, but it was probably groundless, since even a strong military force could not have accomplished this without risking an enormous tumult. The decision reached, Luther's own mood was buoyant. When he came to his lodging, he threw up his hands in triumph with the shout, *Ich bin hindurch, ich bin hindurch*, which one is

tempted to translate into the modern slang, "I've made it!"
And according to a Spanish observer, Luther and his com-
panions "raised their arms, moving the hands and fingers, as the
Germans do for a sign of victory at the tournament."

At eight o'clock the next morning the Emperor himself made
a gesture, and one not unworthy to be matched with Luther's.
Before the assembled Diet he drew attention to the traditions of
loyalty shown by all his ancestors to the Church of Rome, and
recorded his own resolve to support these traditions.

> It is certain that a single friar errs in his opinion, which is
> against what all Christendom has held for over a thousand
> years . . . . To settle this matter I am therefore determined to
> use all my dominions and possessions, my friends, my body,
> my blood, my life and my soul.

And he ended by ordering Luther to be taken back in accordance with his mandate, announcing that thenceforth he would
proceed against him as against a notorious heretic.

The Emperor had thrown down the gauntlet more swiftly
than anyone expected, and thereafter the rest of the Diet
seemed an anticlimax. The Estates got leave to appoint a com-
mission of learned men to reason with Luther, in view of his
offer to accept scriptural proofs of his error. On 24 April this
body duly sent for the friar, who attended along with a Saxon
official and his friends Amsdorf and Jonas. There they encountered the heavily-bearded visage of Duke George, whose fellow
commissioners were the Elector Joachim I of Brandenburg,
Luther's own superior the bishop of Brandenburg, and Richard
Greiffenklau, Archbishop of Trier. These magnates made a
genuine attempt to find a formula, but Luther took the now
familiar line that he would bow to authority so long as he was
not forced to deny the Scriptures.

> I can never make the Lord Christ other than God himself
> made him. If we insist on avoiding offence and hardship, we
> bring them on ourselves in earnest, for the holy Word of God
> has always seemed as if it were about to cause the earth to
> collapse and the heavens to fall.

There followed a private debate with von Eck and Johann

Cochlaeus, the Franconian priest who had formerly supported Luther but from this time stood among his least scrupulous detractors. The debate did not progress far, according to one account because Luther's two adversaries insisted on talking at once and thus prevented him from intervening. There were nevertheless more private interviews, including a frank and ostensibly good-natured one with the Archbishop of Trier, in which Luther refused to promise silence over the doctrines in dispute. In this final conference between Luther and a member of the Roman hierarchy, even conciliatory answers would have had their perils, since according to Aleander the astute von Greiffenklau was seeking to weaken Luther's popularity by tempting him into some minor recantations. He was even prepared to silence him by the gift of a rich priorate.

Given a formal document of dismissal by the Emperor's agents on 25 April, Luther relaxed at an evening party attended by his more distinguished friends in the Diet, and according to Aleander he drank numerous glasses of malmsey, 'to which he is very partial'. The next morning he and other Saxons arranged themselves in two carts and set out on the long journey home. On the way he wrote to the Wittenberg court-painter Lucas Cranach, who was soon to compile so magnificent a record of the Luther circle. This letter contained Martin's own summary of his experiences at the famous Diet of Worms. It read: "Are these your books?" "Yes." "Will you revoke them or not?" "No." "Then get out!" But on the same day he also wrote a more earnest letter to the Emperor, recapitulating his position, giving thanks for his safeconduct and ending with the wholly sincere commendation: "If Christ himself prayed for his enemies on the Cross, how much more should I pray for your Majesty, the Empire, my very dear rulers, and the whole German fatherland." Unplacated, the Emperor and the swiftly dwindling assembly at Worms issued before the end of May an edict placing Luther under the ban of the Empire. The Elector Frederick was left with a conundrum. How should he preserve Luther and yet avoid danger to himself from a papal Interdict or from the Catholic rulers? With much ingenuity he resolved to make Luther disappear for a time.

Just before Luther left Worms, Spalatin told him that, in order to forestall an arrest upon the expiry of the safeconduct, Frederick had decided to have him removed to a secret hiding-place. His comrade Amsdorf also knew this was to happen, but the time and place were not revealed to either. Accordingly, the day after Luther had called on his kinsmen at Möhra, a party of the Elector's horsemen, headed by a trusty knight, intercepted them in the Thuringian Forest. After a mock display of violence and cursing in order to deceive the driver, these agents carried Luther off alone, dressed him as a knight and led him by a roundabout route to the Wartburg, near Eisenach. Here, his whereabouts unknown to the world for several months, he posed as Junker Georg and even grew a beard. In the castle on the crag (which he called according to mood the Kingdom of the Birds or the Isle of Patmos) he settled down again to write, though from time to time harried by depressions with new twists. Sometimes he reproached himself for failing to stage a martyrdom.

> At Worms I let the spirit grow weak within me, instead of rising up as a new Eli against the idols. O, if only I could appear before them again, they would hear some very different things.

At other times there came the opposite thought, one far more agonising.

> My heart trembled. I said to myself: Are you alone right? Are all the rest wrong? Suppose you are the one who is in error! Suppose you are dragging all these souls into error and damnation along with you!

Belief in the saving powers, belief also in the existence of infernal powers, carried him through these dark places.

> I can tell you, in this idle solitude there are a thousand battles with Satan. It is much easier to fight against the incarnate devil—that is, against men—than against spiritual wickedness in the heavenly places.

In the great silent chambers of the Wartburg he suffered hallucinations and fought with his feet and fists against demons

—though the story of the inkpot thrown at the Devil is a legend. Hearing of his sufferings from insomnia and constipation, Spalatin sent him medicines from Wittenberg, but even he could not allay the machinations of the fiend. It remains equally characteristic of Luther that this strange exile did not seriously interrupt his arduous labours.

On the Wartburg he wrote the *Bull on the Last Banquet of our most holy Lord, the Pope,* one of the coarsest of his tracts. But here he also wrote his *Commentary on the Magnificat,* a devoted treatise on the virtues of the Blessed Virgin, whose intercession he beseeches, even while warning his readers against those who put her in the place of God. He began his collection of sermons for the Christian year, which became for many generations the household book of countless pious families. Still more important, he executed his translation of the New Testament, published in September 1522 after he had emerged from retirement. Illustrated by Cranach, the first edition of 3,000 was sold out in three months, but this was nothing compared with the later sales, since over 300 editions appeared in Luther's lifetime. The Old Testament translation was the work of later years, published in four parts, the last in 1534. During the succeeding half-century the Wittenberg press of Hans Lufft alone is thought to have produced 100,000 copies of Luther's Bible.

As the Scriptures dominated the mind of Luther, so Luther's German Bible dominated the social history of the German Reformation. Here and throughout the many lands which accepted his message, the religious movement was ostensibly directed by ordained theologians and preachers, yet it always tended to sweep over the heads of the ecclesiastical establishments and in the last resort it could not be closely controlled by its own promoters. This elemental character of the Reformation arose not merely from social conditions but from the predictable results of scriptural study. Here was not merely an appeal to the Bible but something even more audacious: the placing of the vernacular Scriptures in the hands of any man who could read or merely listen to the reading of a literate neighbour. One did not need to be religious to feel excitement, especially if one felt that here the mighty Church was being put on trial before an even mightier tribunal! The mass sale of the vernacular Scriptures proved the most irrevocable act of the Reformation. The mechanisms of Church and State were not strong enough to withdraw from the peoples what Evangelical naïveté and the printing presses had given them. Contrary to the pathetic suppositions of many early Reformers, Bible-study did not point the way to unanimously accepted conclusions. Yet we should avoid the temptation to attribute all doctrinal brawling to the general dissemination of the Scriptures. In the longer run the latter could serve also as a corrective norm, a rein on irresponsible illuminatism. Moreover, those who anticipated Jean Jacques Rousseau in trusting to the wisdom of peasants gathered under the oak-tree should have begun to sense disillusion even before Luther's Bible came into print. Throughout Germany there were by 1522 thousands of opinionated radicals stimulated by Luther's call for spiritual freedom and all too ready to interpret Holy Writ along lines very different from those suggested by professional theologians, whether Catholic or Lutheran.

In his Bible Luther showed himself a great translator; he created a mountainous landmark in the linguistic and cultural history of his nation, since this book provided the foundation of modern German. Again, whereas the previous German versions had been translations of the Vulgate, Luther's version used the learning of the Renaissance and (with some help from Melanchthon and others) came from the original Hebrew and Greek. Generally speaking, it was a fair and honest translation, even though the term 'congregation' or 'community' (*Gemeinde*) replaced 'church' as an equivalent for *ekklesia*, while the word 'alone' was added—Luther argued that in German it was necessary—after the phrase (*Romans*, iii. 28) 'a main is justified by faith'. Luther strove hard to incorporate the idiom of the people:

> My teachers were the housewife in her home, the children at their games, the merchants in the city squares; I tried to learn from them how to express and explain myself.

As with his subsequent works, he used the linguistic model

furnished by the Saxon Chancery, because it was intelligible to Low Germans and High Germans alike. It is inaccurate to allege that Luther's Bible won instant acceptance throughout the German-speaking world. In the Catholic states a rival translation by Luther's adversary Eck (1537) was long used, while even in Protestant Switzerland the High Alemannic dialect for a time resisted its rivals. But in the end the sheer force of Luther's version surmounted all obstacles and by the seventies the German grammarians were studying and quoting it as a model. Thanks largely to this work the standard language is no longer Upper German, as it had been in the thirteenth century; in essentials it is East Middle German.

Apart from a flying visit to Wittenberg in December (the month in which Melanchthon's *Loci Communes* was published) Luther did not return until early March 1522. During his long absence Carlstadt, Melanchthon and the friar Gabriel Zwilling had introduced a new liturgy, providing an abbreviated and partly German mass, with communion in both kinds for the laity. They had applied the endowments of masses to poor relief, brought monks and nuns out of their cloisters, and even urged them and priests in general to marry. At first shocked by the extension of marriage to former members of religious orders, Luther thought the matter out in the light of the Scriptures and had to admit that he could see no solid objections. The other problems were more difficult. They were epitomised by the ascendancy of Andreas Carlstadt, who now largely controlled the Wittenberg city council and triumphed over the moderates like Melanchthon and Jonas. The conflict between Carlstadt and Luther should not be understood simply as a clash between two equally obstinate and opinionated men of religion. Carlstadt's whole career in many settings shows him to have been one of history's most formidable trouble-makers, as formidable as only a learned and enterprising muddler with some very lucid flashes can be. He had now evolved an ultra-Lutheranism compounded of a puritanical discipline based on the Bible, together with ideas drawn from St. Augustine and from various mystical and sectarian beliefs current in recent centuries. Instead of emphasising faith, he had much to say of

65

Gelassenheit, the abandonment of the soul which makes way for the coming of divine inspiration.

As so often when such leaders seized control, violence had followed. In December the mob, following an earlier example at Erfurt, rioted and destroyed images. Then there arrived the bearded weaver-prophets from Zwickau, whose talk of heavenly visions enraptured the affected Carlstadt, causing him to renounce his academic qualifications and walk around in bare feet as 'Brother Andreas'. Historians have usually associated the rise of Anabaptism with the sectarians who in 1525 grew numerous around Zürich in the shadow of Zwingli. Yet from 1520 this Saxon town of Zwickau, under the leadership of the priest Thomas Müntzer, had witnessed a movement with almost all the same characteristics. A university man and a voracious reader, a far more interesting and original enthusiast than Carlstadt, Müntzer had absorbed the prophetic schemes of Joachim of Fiore, the mystical ideas of the Fraticelli and of Tauler. Through his fellow-prophet Nicholas Storch, who had visited nearby Bohemia, he also inherited Hussite millenarian doctrines. At first he had admired Luther, but was now beginning to denounce him as a 'scribe', an ultra-conservative who put the princes before the poor and the Bible before the promptings of the Spirit. Alongside a considerable biblical knowledge of his own, Müntzer believed in dreams and visions; soon he was to elaborate a curious 'natural theology', based on the notion that a Gospel for simple men could be derived from the Book of Nature.

When this type of radicalism touched Wittenberg itself and started to impress Melanchthon, Luther thought it high time to return, even against the wishes of the Elector. The sheer force of his personality never revealed itself to greater advantage: a week of preaching sufficed to reestablish his own authority and hence the reign of gradualism. His approach to this world of sectarians and individualists seems marked by something more than a self-regarding conservatism. He saw more clearly than the rest that a forcibly established kingdom of the saints must alienate ordinary, sensible men and women from the Gospel. He proposed an inclusive territorial Church to seek the salvation of all men, not a string of cells consisting of self-styled saints or *perfecti*.

> You have gone too fast, for there are brothers and sisters on the other side who belong to us and must still be won. . . . There are some who can run; others must walk, and still others who can hardly creep. Therefore we must not look on our own but on our brother's powers . . . we must first win the hearts of the people. And that is done when I teach only the Word of God, preach only the Word of God, for if you win the heart, you win the whole man.

Yet while these sentiments so swiftly cleared up the outbreak of *Schwärmerei* in the little city of Wittenberg, the hydra sprouted new heads in a hundred other places. Unfamiliar with what seems in our day a general law of revolutions, Luther now found himself locked in a new struggle which made the one at Worms look simple. The radical sectarians had something to say, and their successors would say it more clearly in a later period. But in Luther's day their programmes and purposes were divided and chaotic; they could not offer what the majority of people wanted or needed; some still sought to found the New Jerusalem by the sword and it is no wonder that he saw them merely as dragons to be fought. Like all the other 'moderate' Protestant leaders, he believed that only disaster could result unless he detached his movement from those of the sectarians. These included not only the Anabaptists but Spiritualists or mystics who followed Müntzer in thinking that Luther had substituted a book for the inner light. These latter included Hans Denck and Sebastian Franck, whose writings owe not a little to Luther's early manifestos; another was the attractive Silesian nobleman Caspar Schwenckfeld, for a time among Luther's close friends before he drew apart and somewhat inadvertently founded a sect of his own—one that still exists in America! In the rôle of sorcerer's apprentice, Luther had thus unleashed forces in German society which he could not pretend to direct, and henceforth his religious battle had to be fought on several fronts.

Quite apart from its relation to the religious radicals,

67

Luther's action had played a certain part in energising social forces in themselves little related to religion and quite alien to his spirit. The Imperial knights, who now in 1522–3 made their disastrous bid to master Germany, had marginal connections with his cause. Their wealthy leader Franz von Sickingen had protected clerical adherents of Luther, among them the young Martin Bucer, who obtained a papal release from his vows. The humanist spokesman of the knights Ulrich von Hutten had been prominent among the defenders of both Reuchlin and Luther. Such men more than shared Luther's dislike of the ecclesiastical principalities, which the knights plotted to secularise. Yet few of them can have understood Luther's programme of spiritual regeneration. They put political aims first, but were plainly incapable of governing Germany or of creating the settled conditions amid which Luther's reconstructed churches could prosper. Many had relatives in ecclesiastical chapters and benefices; hence they were not wholly unanimous even in their designs upon the Church. They lacked money and allies; princes and cities feared them as a force of anarchy and refused to back their anticlerical crusade. It was symptomatic that Hutten urged war on the priests by the right of medieval feud. The very poverty which forced the knights to exploit their tenants and serfs prevented them from uniting even the rural population under their command.

Ironically enough, their first intended victim, Luther's recent interrogator Archbishop Greiffenklau of Trier, was himself of knightly extraction and tastes, and he used his considerable military skill to drive them off when in September 1522 they attacked Trier. Joined by the Elector Palatine and Landgrave Philip of Hesse, Greiffenklau then crushed the Rhineland knights, killing Sickingen in May 1523 and driving Hutten to exile and early death in Switzerland. Soon afterwards the Swabian League destroyed the castles and power of the Franconian knights. While this turn of events prevented Luther's movement from being sucked into a vortex of neo-feudal anarchy, it nevertheless preserved the ecclesiastical principalities and allowed the Catholic princes to draw together in opposition. At Regensburg in June 1524 the Emperor's brother

Archduke Ferdinand, together with the Bavarian Dukes and twelve prince-bishops, agreed in the presence of the papal nuncio Campeggio to execute the Edict of Worms against Luther, to fight his heresy and to call for reforms of discipline and doctrine in the Church. This meeting we might see as the political Counter Reformation in embryo.

The Peasant's War of 1524-5 cannot in any large degree be ascribed to Luther's teaching, yet it derived a certain stimulus from the atmosphere he had created, and it exposed Lutheranism to fresh risks and tensions: These ill-coordinated rebellions in south-western and central Germany were primarily directed against the growing oppressions of landlords and were strengthened by the example of the Swiss, who had long ago thrown territorial princes and great ecclesiastical landowners off their backs. The *Bundschuh* movements – so called after their badge, the tied shoe of the peasant as opposed to the riding-boot of the squire – had raged sporadically from about 1493 to 1517. From that point Luther's attack on the corruptions of the Church, his general denunciation of social injustice and abuses, had helped to add doctrinaire elements to this economic discontent. That his outbursts on the freedom of a Christian were misunderstood by the peasants did not weaken their effect. When his former admirers Müntzer and Carlstadt became involved with the peasant agitators, Luther found his own movement deeply compromised. His need to oppose these men and to be seen opposing them became correspondingly urgent. In August 1524 he made a preaching tour of the Saale Valley to counter their efforts, came up with Carlstadt in the Black Bear at Jena, and tossed his adversary a golden guilder, the traditional challenge to scholarly combat. About the same time he published his tract *Against the Heavenly Prophets*, ridiculing without mercy the extravagances of religious radicalism.

From his new base at Mühlhausen Müntzer failed substantially to recreate the centuries-old tradition of popular millenarianism; had he succeeded, his praises would hardly have been sung by Engels, or his memory kept green in Marxist mythology. The famous *Twelve Articles of the Peasantry* show a moderation perhaps in part attributable to the conservative

69

social teaching of Luther; they assert the need for obedience to legitimate government and for the acceptance of social rank and class, even when serfdom itself shall be abolished. Their religious demands – that congregations should freely elect their ministers and that the latter must preach the Gospel plainly and without additions – were by no means inharmonious with the views of Luther. Nevertheless, the peasants failed to win substantial support from the other orders of society. At Heilbronn, Rothenburg, Bamberg, Würzburg and some small towns in Thuringia artisans joined the movement, yet in general the peasants and the unprivileged townsmen failed to cooperate effectively, since in detail their grievances were so different. Again, the peasants failed to rise everywhere: the north-east, the north-west, nearly all Bavaria and the lands of most Imperial cities remained untouched. That the proletarian movement failed to present a national front, to produce a great leader, to create administrative organs or even a theocracy; these were negative factors of great importance to Luther's movement. They also spelt the military failure of the peasants. A series of local victories by Philip of Hesse and the Swabian League was followed by the final rout of the main rebel force at Frankenhausen on 15 May 1525. Two days afterwards Müntzer was found and executed amid a mass slaughter which dwarfed the other cataclysms of the age. Carlstadt had managed to extricate himself just before Frankenhausen by being lowered in secret from the walls of Rothenburg. To escape the consequences he made a grovelling appeal to Luther, who generously gave him and his family asylum in his own house.

The severity of Luther's language against the peasants has rightly been regarded as a major blot upon the record of a Christian leader. His first response to the revolt was in fact different. His *Admonitions for Peace on the Twelve Articles* declares both sides in the wrong and in danger of damnation; it urges the lords to make equitable concessions while it denies the right of the peasants to revolt. The latter he accuses of perverting the Gospel to worldly ends; Christian liberty is a spiritual thing and the affairs of God's kingdom must be kept apart from those of the world. Luther in fact believed that even serfdom could be justified from the Bible. Courageously, he went out to preach in the disordered countryside and narrowly escaped being done to death by the rebels at Nordhausen. For a time he even thought the peasants might win and anarchy be perpetuated. Hence in his pamphlet *Against the Thieving and Murderous Gangs of Peasants* (May 1525) he dropped moderation and in hysterical language urged the princes to kill the rebels without mercy 'as one must kill a mad dog'. It should be added that after Frankenhausen he again appealed for clemency and called down the judgment of God upon the slaughterers of the defeated rebels. On the other hand, in later years he did not retract his more violent gestures and continued to defend the substantial justice of his opinions. These were indeed the opinions of nearly all the 'responsible' men of the ruling and middle classes throughout Europe, who believed social hierarchy to be divinely ordained, lived in terror of anarchy, and thought no fate bad enough for rebels, especially proletarian rebels. Luther's violence doubtless weakened his hold on the peasantry, many of whom thenceforth tended to class Luther with the old priests, to fall into apathy or succumb to the preaching of the sectarians. On the grounds of worldly wisdom alone, it would have been better to leave the butchery to the princes, who, as Luther soon found to his dismay, could be relied upon to extend it far beyond the bounds of military necessity.

From this last judgment we can at least except the Elector Frederick, who died during the course of the revolt, bewailing the errors of the ruling classes and urging the need for peaceful mediation. His death proved no disaster for Luther, who continued to receive loyal backing from his brother and successor the Elector John (1525-32) and then from the latter's son John Frederick (1532-54), an ardent disciple who for years had avidly read Luther's works as they came from the press. At first Luther regarded John Frederick as a light-weight, but in the end this steadfast if bibulous and rather stupid prince was to prove a greater credit to him than the rest.

The removal of the knights and the peasants from the Imperial chessboard simplified the Reformer's situation in regard to German society, but it did nothing to decrease his dependence upon the princes. Some critics have even suggested that as the offspring of a small *entrepreneur* Luther behaved like any member of his class, one which tended to link with the princes against common enemies: peasants, sectarians, robber-knights and city bankers. Yet this doctrinaire class-interpretation does not closely fit the recorded Luther. That he was consciously concerned with religion and ethics (and seldom with anything else) will not be disputed by anyone familiar with Luther's mind. In all sincerity he denied the subject's right to revolt upon biblical grounds. But so far from being a blind prince-worshipper, he often scourged the princes in speech and writing. Of irrational, inherited class prejudices he was more free than most of his contemporaries. His implicit trust lay in the Word, not in any human political agency but in the irresistible, self-revealing activity of God, which operates through preaching, prayer and Bible-study. As he saw his doctrines surging across Germany, he felt good reason to regard himself as the chosen instrument of this force.

The Word did it all. Had I wished I could have started a conflagration at Worms. But while I sat still and drank beer with Philip and Amsdorf, God dealt the Papacy a mighty blow.

During these earlier stages such a belief relegated the political mechanisms, even ecclesiastical organisation itself, to a lowly place on the agenda, for it seemed that neither could accomplish much, except perhaps to remove some of the mundane obstacles to the Word. In any case, Luther thought it unlikely that God would suffer the wicked world to endure much longer. His political conservatism did not in fact exalt the princes alone; it placed them within the context of Imperial institutions and under the overlordship of the Emperor. Like almost every German of his day, even the rebellious peasants, Luther sought to retain the structure of the Empire, as well as the territorial governments which operated within its framework. Until 1530, when his hand was forced, he tried to restrain the princes from taking arms against the Emperor. To the end of his days, and with an extraordinary lack of political realism, he continued to speak of the latter with reverence, to hope against hope that Charles was not irrevocably committed to the overthrow of Evangelical religion.

The ridicule commonly directed by non-German writers against the cumbrous institutions of the Holy Roman Empire can make us grossly underestimate the grip of Imperial ideas upon Luther's contemporaries. What we tend to dismiss in Luther as arch-conservatism was a normal loyalty and discipline, though perhaps expressed by him in unusually religious terms. Luther was governed neither by hypocrisy nor by anything resembling modern class-loyalties. If in the event he drove a wedge between Emperor and princes, it was the last thing he wanted to do. But as circumstances demanded practical organisation, as he was forced to become a more active agent of the Word, upon whom could he rely save on his prince and that prince's allies? The Emperor proved no mediator but a hostile partisan. The cities contained a host of valuable allies but they cooperated uneasily with each other, and hence developed no decisive military strength. They ruled too little of the countryside and in terms of population most were very small. Luther could not appeal with much hope to the prince-bishops, the knights, the humanists, the peasants, the long-bearded millenarians. He was a German, the subject of a powerful Elector who alone could protect him and let him deliver his religious message. He could not much alter the shape of his political world. It was given to him, just as the Word itself was given.

Whatever harm had been done by Luther's sanguinary phrases, his movement continued to expand with impressive force. In July 1525, a year after the meeting of the southern Catholic princes at Regensburg, an alliance was also concluded by the northern Catholic princes, among them George of Saxony, Joachim of Brandenburg, Henry Duke of Wolfenbüttel and Eric Duke of Brunswick. Nevertheless, in later years nearly all these northern states were to turn Protestant. Already Electoral Saxony was finding strong politico-religious allies. Philip of Hesse, whose unfortunate amours did not exclude a certain personal piety, declared for the new faith in 1525; in the following year he established Protestantism in his territory and made a close agreement with the Saxon Elector to collaborate in its defence. To the cause Philip brought his military skill and much political courage: he believed in the secular sword and it was not his fault if the Protestant divines pontificated and haggled over the theology of the eucharist instead of swallowing their differences and so furthering political alliances. Also in 1525 Albert of Hohenzollern, Grand Master of the Teutonic Knights and a vassal of Poland, took Luther's advice, laid aside his clerical office, made himself Duke of Prussia and carried through a sweeping programme of reform in his territory. His geographical situation and his marriage to a Danish princess soon furthered the extension of the movement to Scandinavia. Another Hohenzollern Prince, Casimir of Ansbach, a close neighbour of the great city of Nuremberg, also stood among Luther's early converts.

At the easiest of times it would not have proved a simple task for the Habsburgs to defeat these Evangelical princes and occupy their territories, the more especially since few if any of the Catholic rulers would have lent themselves to such an Imperial crusade. But after Worms the Habsburgs found their hands also fettered by external events. Charles himself immediately left Germany to fight the French: soon afterwards he went on to Spain, where so much needed to be done, and he did not revisit the Empire until 1530. His Netherlandish, Burgundian and Italian inheritances involved him in alternately hot and cold war with France, and hence made France a natural ally of his opponents, both Lutheran and Turkish. Meanwhile his brother Archduke Ferdinand, appointed regent of all the German Habsburg lands, became by marriage to Anne of Poland heir to the Jagiellon kingdoms of Bohemia and Hungary. These the Archduke inherited in 1526 when his brother-in-law King Louis died fighting the Turks at Mohács. King Ferdinand was thenceforth dragged into a complex struggle to assert his rights both against the Infidel and against rival Christian princes in Transylvania. In 1529 the Turks stood for a time at the gates of Vienna, and though he pushed them back he could establish his rule only in a narrow strip of western

Hungary. Thus Habsburg attentions were diverted to the western, eastern and southern peripheries of the Empire, while Luther consolidated his grip at the centre and in the north. This inability of the Habsburgs to assemble their military potential and throw it against the Lutheran princes was in fact to last until the very year of Luther's death.

Nevertheless, those historians who have described the early triumphs of Lutheranism merely in terms of military power and princely intrigue have succumbed to the worst of all their vocational diseases: political monomania. In no country was the soil of the Reformation irrigated through princely channels alone. To many communities the new religious notions were brought, with or without governmental consent, by missionaries and booksellers. Ideas both Lutheran and sectarian flourished independently in the minds of simple and educated people. The flood of ideas overflowed the channels cut by princes. In Wittenberg itself Luther received firm backing from a remarkably talented and zealous group of colleagues and pupils; never in European history did the staff of one small university play so mighty a rôle in a major movement of thought. Fame was bringing new recruits. Even by the summer of 1519 Wittenberg, until recently obscure, had nearly as many students as the largest German universities. During the twenties Luther was represented by eminent preachers and theologians in many centres, by Johann Lang at Erfurt, Johannes Brenz at Schwäbisch Hall, Oswald Myconius at Gotha, Andreas Osiander at Nuremberg, Nicholas Amsdorf at Magdeburg. Determined agents were setting out for the far-flung communities of Baltic Europe; others would soon link with the Hussites of Bohemia and Moravia and cross the mountains into the great plains of Hungary. The early missionary history of Lutheranism should not be unduly obscured by the personal story of Luther; ever inspired from Wittenberg, it remains in its own right an achievement worthy to be ranked alongside the miracles of propaganda later wrought by the Society of Jesus.

One aspect of this expansion, the production and dissemination of Lutheran literature, created a wholly new phenomenon in history. And to find adequate comparisons one must perhaps look ahead to the age of Voltaire. Luther's thirty publications between 1517 and 1520 probably sold over a third of a million copies. Each of the great tracts of 1520 immediately ran through fifteen to eighteen editions. It has been calculated that in the single year 1523 as many as 183 books were published in Luther's name, plus some further 215 books by other writers favourable to the Reformation. During that same year, however, scarcely more than twenty books can be enumerated on the Catholic side. This great output of Protestant propaganda was applied to relatively small populations, to people with distractions less complex than those of our day. Enlivened in many cases by vivid engravings, often read aloud to several people at once, the potency of a single copy could no doubt have been great. The fact that Lutheranism was not merely imposed from above by princes can also be seen from its early successes in the German cities, where people were more obviously accepting it under their own volition. By 1524–5, though the big advance had yet to come, Lutheranism had already won predominance at Erfurt, Gotha, Magdeburg, Nuremberg, Bremen, Stettin, Altenburg and a host of lesser towns. Further off, it was being welcomed at places as different as Frankfurt-am-Main, Schwäbisch Hall and Ulm. Elsewhere, as at Jena and even in conservative Cologne, there were radical stirrings inspired by Carlstadt as well as by Luther. In the proud Imperial city of Strassburg on the Rhineland plain and again in Zürich, the chief city of the Swiss Confederation, movements largely independent of Luther's direct influence had arisen.

In Strassburg the Reformation effectively began in 1521 with the sermons of Matthew Zell in the cathedral. When he was refused access to the great stone pulpit, the gild of carpenters made him a wooden one, around which large congregations continued to assemble. In May 1523 there arrived that highly academic figure Wolfgang Capito, a noted hebraist, one of the collaborators of Erasmus, a former professor of Basle and chaplain to Archbishop Albert of Mainz. Somewhat surprisingly, he was soon captivated by the enthusiasm of Zell. At the same time they were joined by Sickingen's former chaplain Martin Bucer, who in the subsequent years worked his way to the leadership through sheer ability as preacher, writer and liturgist. These clerics and others formed a close-knit group with the lay magistrates, headed by Strassburg's famed statesman Jakob Sturm. The Strassburg Reformation, which swiftly spread to the lesser towns of Alsace, owed much to the initiative of Luther, yet it soon diverged from Wittenberg in many respects. Among its special features Bucer's liturgical experiments and theological speculations were perhaps not the most significant. Like Zwingli and the Swiss Reformers, Strassburg gave considerable powers to the lay elders of the Church; its example helped to inspire the social organisation of religion in the Geneva of Calvin, who was to spend the important years 1538–41 with Bucer at Strassburg. Again, the Strassburgers behaved more liberally than Luther toward the radical sects, even toward the Anabaptists, who in their thousands resorted to Strassburg to escape persecution. Too often obscured from historians by Wittenberg, Zürich and Geneva, this became the great city of refuge, of practical Christianity, of ecumenical idealism, the city to visit in imagination if one would realise the rich complexity of the forces released in Europe by Luther's revolt.

Under the mediating theologian Bucer, and also through its geographical situation, Strassburg was well fitted to undertake the coordination of the Saxon with the Swiss movement. The rapid estrangement of the two offered no comfort to men who lacked Luther's trust in an all-providing Deity. Though Luther was already famous when Zwingli began his movement in Zürich, the latter had already been dreaming of a scriptural Reformation when he first heard of Luther's efforts in 1518–19. He was at least sincere when he wrote, "I have not learnt the teachings of Christ from Luther but from the very Word of God". Zwingli was a manly, forthright Christian warrior who had never undergone Luther's desolating experiences. An enthusiastic humanist, a believer in the salvation of the great pagan men of virtue, a disciple of Erasmus, he burned with the desire to translate Erasmian criticism into practical reforms. From the time of his installation in 1518 as people's priest of the Great Minster at Zürich he was evolving a theology in some respects more radical than that of Luther. Accepting the latter on justification and predestination, he stood starkly opposed in his doctrine of the mass. The words 'This is my body' he took to mean 'This signifies my body', and like the later Wycliffites he embraced a symbolic or figurative interpretation of the sacrament. Having more than a streak of rationalism and a strong sense of the gap between matter and spirit, Zwingli rejected the notion that grace could be conveyed through material objects. And more readily than Luther he entered into active partnership with the secular State, joining hands with the lay magistrates of Zürich in order to erect a system of Christian education and discipline. The other leading Swiss cities soon began to follow his lead. Toward the end of 1522 Johann Hussgen (called Oecolampadius) arrived in Basle and soon led the city into a Reformation parallel with that of Zürich. In Bern the movement similarly dates from the early twenties, particularly with the preaching of Berchtold Haller.

The Swiss Reformers would hardly have echoed Luther's saying, that even as he sat drinking beer with Philip and Amsdorf the Word would regenerate sinful human society. And in regard to the instruments of Reformation, they proved that a city council suitably manned by keen Bible-students could go to work more swiftly than any German prince. These prudent and practical Swiss accepted the need for a stronger ecclesiastical discipline. In default of the hard channels provided by such discipline, there seemed to them every likelihood that the springs of the Reformation would run out upon the sands of religious subjectivism and individualism. These aberrations they could witness to perfection at home, for the chief scource of Anabaptism was the Zürich area. Here in 1524–5 Grebel, Mantz and Blaurock rejected the authority of Zwingli, began baptising adults in the rivers and holding simplified communion services. From thence the sect spread with astounding speed into south Germany, Tyrol, Austria, Moravia; into the Netherlands on the one hand and across Poland on the other. Its essence lay in discipleship, in the notion of withdrawn communities of saints standing apart from the godless mass of mankind. Though it lacked any closely-agreed programme, a few positions afforded some common ground amid the welter of radical beliefs: baptism for adult converts only; strict excommunication of unregenerate offenders; an attempt literally to live like the first Christians; the renunciation of warfare and of public office; the allowance of a rôle in salvation to human free-will. The last of these principles caused Lutherans, Zwinglians, and later on Calvinists to denounce the Anabaptists as guilty of the Pelagian heresy. To these sectarians Zwingli opposed a stern opposition and the city of Zürich was amongst the first states to confront them with the death penalty. Luther on the other hand regarded the Zwinglians themselves as all too little removed in doctrine from the Anabaptists. He tended always to lump together all those to the left of his own conservative theology; in particular his attachment to a Real Presence in the mass ruled out any cool examination of Zwinglian tenets.

One feature of sectarian influence Luther particularly feared and hated: the belief encouraged by Carlstadt that scholarship and formal education were useless in this brave new world of exciting spiritual revelations. While Luther was still in the Wartburg the Elector Frederick and others observed that many students were forsaking Wittenberg and other universities on this plea. Having himself submitted to the drudgery of Greek and Hebrew, Luther had come to prize the humanities as indispensable for biblical study and for the whole defence of Evangelical religion. Though prepared to abandon the old philosophy and theology, he could not afford to abandon these modern weapons—even less so, as he looked around and saw the appalling results of unlearned illuminatism. In March 1523 he wrote to Eobanus:

> Do not give way to your fear, lest we Germans become more barbarous than ever, by reason of the decline of letters through our theology. I am persuaded that, without an expert training in literary studies, no true theology can establish and maintain itself, seeing that in former times it has always fallen miserably and lain prostrate with the decline and fall of learning. On the other hand, it is unquestionable that there has never been a clear revelation of divine truth unless the way has been prepared—as if by a John the Baptist—

through the revival and practice of the study of languages and literature. Surely, there is nothing I should less desire to happen than that our young men should neglect poetry and rhetoric [i.e. humanist studies] . . . . Wherefore I beg you to urge the students of Erfurt to devote themselves strenuously to this study.

Whatever modern historians may think, Luther did not believe that Renaissance and Reformation were in all respects mutually antagonistic movements. He clearly perceived that the fate of a religion expressed in books and ideas, rather than in images and theatrical presentation, must depend on a general advance of literacy at all levels. A year later he is writing to a friend at Eisenach:

I beseech you, do your utmost in the cause of the training of young people, for I am convinced that the neglect of education will bring the greatest ruin to the Gospel. This matter is the most important of all.

Luther's fight against official parsimony, public utilitarianism and anti-intellectual movements in religion reached its climax early in 1524, when he published his appeal *To the Councillors of all the Towns in Germany, that they should establish Christian Schools*. This tract Ranke compared in importance with the address *To the Christian Nobility*. In it Luther bids the towns realise that a shortage of sound education is a worse enemy to the commonwealth than the Turk. If a town gives a guilder to defend the Empire, it should give a hundred to make one boy into an educated man. If it spends readily on fortifications and improvements, why should it grudge spending on schoolmasters? Along with the Gospel, God has provided a multitude of teachers, far more skilled than the pedants who years ago made asses and blockheads of us all. Town councils should not rest content merely to establish elementary schools to teach German and the Bible. Christianity was first revealed in the ancient languages, and higher education must not be neglected, or Germany will both lose the Gospel and deserve to be called a barbarian land. Hereabouts Luther naïvely supposes that God allowed Greece to be overrun by the Turks in order that by the flight of the Greeks Europe should be instructed in the language of the New Testament. Aided by this revival of learning, he claims, we now have the Gospel in as authentic a form as the Apostles had it. Luther prizes St. Bernard above all other doctors of the Church, but St. Bernard (and still more St. Augustine) would have been preserved from many errors of interpretation had they possessed our modern linguistic skills. "As the sun is to the shadow, so is a knowledge of the original texts to all the commentaries of the Fathers."

Luther demands much more from the schools and universities than the training of the new race of clergy. We must not, he continues, despise the utilitarian importance of education to both sexes and to society at large.

It is reason enough for establishing the best possible schools for boys and girls, that the State (for its own well-being) needs well-educated men and women for the better government of land and people, and for the proper nurture of children in the home.

To make teaching generally effective we must rid the system of its dull memorising and flogging. In embittered terms, Luther then recalls the martyrdom of his own school-days and wishes he had then been given the chance to study the poets and the historians. He does not, of course, demand this higher education for all. Yet he would have the towns also provide a sound elementary education, linked with some practical training in a useful craft, and make it compulsory for every boy and girl. With equal prescience, he urges the foundation of public libraries in all the towns. He would fill the shelves with genuinely serviceable books, but exclude material on canon law, scholastic theology and philosophy. In place of all this 'filth', he would provide bibles in the original tongues and in translation, the best of the ancient commentators, the classical authors both pagan and Christian, the best works on law, medicine and on all the arts and sciences. To these he would add histories and chronicles in the various languages, but particularly those relating to German national history, since in history we can learn something of the will of God expressed in the acts of men.

These decades are notable throughout Europe for a number of fine treatises on education, but even alongside the best of them Luther's manifesto remains impressive in its practicality and breadth of view. His enemies were unfair in dismissing it as a guilty afterthought, because Luther had at least begun talking along these lines in 1520, before the eruption of the sectarians. Neither was his tract a mere façade of theory. Luther and Bugenhagen were already reorganising the schools of Wittenberg, which had been closed during the troubles of 1521-2, while within a year of Luther's appeal to the towns, schools were being founded or revived on Evangelical lines at Magdeburg, Halberstadt, Nordhausen, Gotha, Eisleben and Nuremberg. In 1527 Philip of Hesse established at Marburg the first university to be founded under Protestant auspices. Meantime Melanchthon was earning the proud title *praeceptor Germaniae*. The last criticism which could be brought against the Reformation (or the Counter-Reformation) is a lack of interest in those educational advances for which sixteenth-century Europe showed so laudable an enthusiasm. Misled by the initial confusion, Erasmus made one of his major blunders when he wrote, "Wherever Lutheranism prevails, there the destruction of letters takes place".

It was in fact about this same time that Luther and Erasmus decisively drew asunder. We have already observed that the two had begun to sense their incompatibility in 1517, even though they were still exchanging civilities in 1520. The delicate sense of irony, the sceptical questioning, the cautious, rather feline regard for his own comfort, these Erasmian traits found no echo in the earnest soul of Luther, who thought Erasmus 'as slippery as an eel'. He could never have asked the question or given the reply of Erasmus: "Is it worth overturning the world for the sake of truth? Sometimes silence is better. Jesus was silent before Herod!" The heir of the Platonists, Erasmus believed men were created in the image of God and, though they needed faith and grace for their full development, did not lack a natural inclination toward goodness and beauty. This tranquil faith based on reason and personal virtues could be fostered even by the great pagan models; it had nothing in common with the tragic convictions of Luther, with the masked God whose ways are not ours, or with the lost sinner, incapable of self-help, wholly infected by an ingrowing selfhood, dependent solely on election by the Almighty. The immensity of this division was unrealised by the people of Europe. Until 1521, perhaps years later, many men thought of the two mighty figures as paladins united in one glorious cause. When Luther disappeared into the Wartburg, someone told Albrecht Dürer, then in Antwerp, that he had been arrested and imprisoned. The artist immediately penned in his diary a long and impassioned diatribe bewailing the fate of the Reformer and calling on Erasmus to rise up as a knight of Christ and grasp the martyr's crown in desperate combat with the forces of tyranny and darkness.

So far from adopting this heroic stance, Erasmus was soon listening to Pope Adrian VI and to King Henry VIII, for both invited him to enter the lists against Luther. He was also driven on by the enmity of Aleander and other conservative divines, who would dearly have liked to nail him down upon charges of heresy. Finally in 1524 he produced his *Diatribe on Free Will*, an elegantly-phrased pot-boiler described by Luther in his characteristic banter:

> My heart went out to you for having defiled your lovely, brilliant flow of language with so much vile stuff. I thought it outrageous to convey material of so low a quality in the trappings of such rare eloquence; it is like using gold or silver dishes to carry garden rubbish or manure.

Erasmus, superficial theologian as he was, calls forth an answering chord in any civilised man; he wanted Christianity with a minimum of cocksure dogmatising, and he regarded these problems of divine grace and human free-will as among the vainer theological and philosophical disputes. Divested of its humanist tinsel, his doctrine in the *Diatribe* follows familiar Occamist lines by no means acceptable to subsequent Catholic theologians. The human will boasts a distinct if feeble power toward salvation, whereby man earns 'congruent' merit of God. By exerting this power a man becomes a fit subject to receive that internal grace which a just God—though not bound to give it—does in fact bestow on such men. Once armed with this grace, a man can do good works far beyond his former ability. By doing them he now attains 'condign' merit, which puts God under a certain obligation to reward him.

Luther's reply to the *Diatribe*, published in December 1525, was the famous treatise *De Servo Arbitrio*, now usually translated *The Bondage of the Will*. This is an altogether more professional performance: it constitutes Luther's greatest single intellectual achievement and his most sustained essay in systematic theology. Luther himself later said that none of his works deserved preservation except this and his shorter *Catechism*. Unlike Erasmus, he cared passionately about these particular doctrines. With consummate skill he took each text used by Erasmus and destroyed the interpretation placed upon it. The conflict serves to discourage the popular notion of Erasmus the broad rationalist, as opposed to Luther the rough monomaniac. Here the boot is on the other foot; the contest is unequal because it lies wholly within Luther's own province.

Luther's alleged denigration of 'reason' and of free-will has often been misunderstood. He never impugned rational consistency in argument: he merely said that human reason should keep to its appointed sphere, and not vainly seek to penetrate the abysses God keeps secret from man in this life. Again, in denying free-will Luther does not make man an automaton: he asserts the psychological freedom of man in respect to 'things below him'; man has freedom to do good works, to obey the laws of states, even the moral law. His unfreedom lies in the fact that he cannot turn to God, satisfy God by his performance, or play the slightest part in the process leading to his own salvation. Luther uses the Bible to sweep away all ideas of human merit, congruent and condign alike. The supposedly modified Pelagianism of Erasmus is worse to him than the original heresy, because it seeks to cheapen divine standards by supposing God to be satisfied by a very feeble motion of man toward him. Either man contributes independently to his own salvation or he does not; but the Bible makes it clear that the whole of the work is that of God, through Christ. God is really omnipotent;

he pervades and energises the whole universe; his immutable sovereign will governs all his creatures; he causes even the first turning of man toward faith. God does not, as Erasmus thinks, strengthen a will which has already started in the right direction of its own accord. His action is a total saving of corrupt nature.

In his unregenerate state, says Luther, man is like a horse standing between two riders, God and Satan. Though falsely imagining himself to be his own master, he cannot choose which of these riders will ride him. Yet in the last resort Satan himself only rides man by permission of God. Under the divine sovereignty nothing happens by chance. God is no mere detached spectator of man's struggle; he has not created the universe and then 'gone off to the land of the Moors for a drink, as Homer writes of Jupiter'.

> How else can you believe confidently, trust in, and depend upon God's promises . . . ? For the greatest and only consolation of Christians is knowing that God does not lie, does all things immutably, and that his will cannot be resisted, changed or hindered.

So absolute a definition of divine omnipotence must obviously carry disturbing implications, and no one of that age was more keenly aware of them than Luther. He agrees with Erasmus that at first sight it may well seem as if 'God delights in the torment of poor wretches, and is a fitter object for our hate than for our love'.

> If I could by any means understand how this same God, who makes such a show of wrath and unrighteousness, can yet be merciful and just, there would be no need for faith. But as it is, the impossibility of understanding makes room for the exercise of faith . . . . Doubtless it gives the greatest possible offence to commonsense or natural reason, that God, who is proclaimed as being full of mercy and goodness, and so on, should of his own mere will abandon, harden and damn men . . . . and it is this that has been a stumbling-block to so many great men down the ages. And who would not stumble at it? I have stumbled at it myself more than once, down to the deepest pit of despair, so that I wished I had never been

made a man. (That was before I knew how health-giving that despair was, and how close to grace.) This is why so much toil and trouble has been devoted to clearing the goodness of God and throwing the blame on man's will.

Luther thus places the whole onus on the sovereign will of God. His practical advice is simple. Abstain from curious enquiry as to God's hidden purposes, and concentrate on what God has revealed in Christ. Remember that though men on earth cannot fully apprehend the divine intention, they may hope to understand it in the future life. Men should keep in mind the 'three lights' of nature, grace and glory. By the light of nature we cannot, for example, understand why the good suffer and the bad prosper, yet by the light of grace (which reveals the rectifying process of the next life) this anomaly can be understood. Yet even by the light of grace we cannot answer this more difficult question: why does God damn men who by their own strength can do nothing but sin? This apparent paradox we shall understand only by the light of glory in the life to come. Meanwhile we must believe aright according to Scriptural doctrine; we must not shuffle out of our difficulties on the absurd basis of salvation through human merits, through the exercise of a saving free-will.

This then is the austere and tragic doctrine deduced from St. Paul and stamped by Luther for good or ill upon the heart of Protestantism. Yet needless to add, there were from the first less hardy Lutherans who wanted to have the cake of divine omnipotence and to devour it at the same time; they were soon to reintroduce elements of self-salvation little different from those maintained by Erasmus.

Despite the high value he attached to the literary aspects of humanism, from 1525 Luther often showed his awareness of the cosmic distances separating his doctrine of man from that of the Erasmians. In the *Table Talk* he is recorded as saying, "I consider Erasmus to be the greatest enemy Christ has had these thousand years past." In this bitter leave-taking there lay more than any mere personal rancour against the lost leader; there lay all the tension that still exists between the two poles of our western culture.

Chapter Five

Lutheranism in Germany,
1525–*c*.1540

IN the year 1525 Luther's private life entered a wholly new phase on account of his marriage. The circumstances leading to this event have a rather comic charm. Two years earlier a dozen nuns from the Cistercian convent at Nimbschen near Grimma had been converted to the new faith and sought Luther's advice. The abduction of nuns from their convents still carried severe penalties in law, but he nevertheless arranged that they should be brought out by an elderly merchant of Torgau, who had perfect facilities for the operation, since he regularly delivered barrels of herrings to the nunnery in a covered wagon. When at last nine of the ladies arrived in Wittenberg, one of Luther's students wrote to a friend, "A cart-load of vestal virgins has just arrived in town, all more eager for marriage than for life itself. God grant them husbands lest something worse should happen!" To this laudable purpose Luther bestirred himself and in due course all were married off except the spirited gentlewoman Katherine von Bora, who lived in the household of Lucas Cranach. Martin assigned her first to Jerome Baumgärtner, a student from a Nuremberg patrician family, and then to Dr. Glatz, a former rector of the University, whom she refused even though in those days at the age of 26 a woman's chances of marriage were often thought small.

Since 1521 numerous clerical marriages had taken place in Saxony, but the obvious way out did not at first suggest itself to Luther. He had already reached the age of 42 without contemplating matrimony, and only his most imaginative calumniators have suggested that he was subject to violent sexual impulses. No doubt he could have married earlier, though the step might possibly have displeased the Elector. Certainly, as a heretic under the ban, he at first felt himself in no position to embark on family life. When Katherine herself boldly told his friend Amsdorf that she would marry either him or Amsdorf, Martin did not at first take the idea seriously. Though he said later that he changed his mind partly in order to please his father, one can hardly believe that this was the decisive influence. He seems at last to have concluded that he should set a personal example by spiting the devil and defying the taboo still widely attached to clerical marriage. He even thought that his gesture might encourage his old adversary Archbishop Albert of Mainz to do likewise, since at this time Albert contemplated turning himself into a secular prince. If in any modern sense Luther can be said to have fallen in love, he did this, like so many men of his day, not before but after marriage.

The public betrothal between Martin and Katherine took place on 13 June 1525; the wedding ceremony came a fortnight later and was followed by a dinner in the Augustinian cloister and a dance in the town hall. That very evening the proceedings were complicated by the arrival of Carlstadt in flight from the wrath of the princes, but the Luthers tolerantly afforded shelter to him and his family. At this moment they were far from opulent. Katherine's mother was dead, while her father had remarried and refused to accept further responsibilities toward her. Luther's academic stipend was small and he never drew royalties from his publications. But erelong the new Elector behaved handsomely; he not only raised Luther's salary but gave the Black Cloister of the Augustinians as a dwelling-house to the newly-married couple. Amongst the unexpected wedding gifts was one sent to Katherine by the gallant Archbishop Albert himself; it took the form of twenty golden guilders, and though Luther thought she ought to decline them, no doubt she had more sense.

These tentative, prosaic beginnings led easily into an affectionate and successful partnership. Domestic labour was available in plenty even for people of moderate means, and Katherine showed herself a prodigious worker and an excellent manager. She had need of these qualities, since her husband took no thought for money; he entertained readily and gave generously. He did indeed try to play the prudent father and started growing melons, cucumbers, radishes and other produce in the garden. For a time he even learned the craft of wood-turning, remarking that the day might come when he would be forced to depend on manual labour. But meanwhile, and more effectively, Katherine kept poultry, pigs and cows, managed an orchard and later on acquired a little farm at Zulsdorf nearby. She also brewed beer, which Luther drank philosophically when he could not afford a consignment of anything better. One of his letters is addressed 'To my beloved wife Katherine, Mrs. Dr. Luther, mistress of the pig-market, Lady of Zulsdorf, and whatever other titles may befit Your Grace'. On another occasion he called her 'the Morning Star of Wittenberg, because she was up and had her kitchen fire alight long before anybody else in the town. They took in student-boarders, some of whom had their notebooks ever at hand to take down those tumul-tuous, ever-varied, often brilliant, sometimes pig-headed mono-logues which later emerged in print as the *Table Talk*. Perhaps a shade annoyed at the way he pontificated and attracted all the limelight, Katherine said he should charge them extra for these unofficial lectures delivered during mealtimes. But she was fully aware that she had married a great man and had thereby accepted responsibilities beyond those of the average housewife.

No doubt she prolonged Luther's life. He tells us that before his marriage his bed was not made for a year on end, and that worn out by labour he had tumbled into it without even notic-ing the disorder. Like many high-geared and effective people, he suffered from a variety of ailments, and she tended them all with an excellent knowledge of home-remedies which Luther sadly missed during his absences from Wittenberg. As time passed his affection deepened and he abandoned his former Pauline view that marriage was a remedy against sin. Coming between the clerical nonsense of the middle ages and the romantic nonsense of recent times, his views on family life helped to inaugurate attitudes more sensible than either. His acceptance of the patriarchal notions of his day was softened by an unexpected but immense fund of gentleness and affection. Luther was at his best with children: for them he composed charming rhymes and carols, while the imaginative fairy-story he wrote for his four-year-old son could hardly have been bettered by Charles Lamb. And these things came from the pen of one who dealt the hardest literary knocks of a hard-hitting century! At home the contentious ex-monk somehow achieved the right blend of patience and humour. His household soon became as famed throughout Europe as that of Thomas More, and both helped to establish the dignity of family life for a generation which was ceasing to glorify celibacy. When the neighbours laughed to see a father hanging out the diapers, he retorted "Let them laugh. God and the angels are smiling in heaven." He reflected on Christ's saying that we must become as little children, looked at his own and burst out "Dear God, this is too much; have we really got to become such idiots?" The Luthers had six children born between 1526 and 1534: three sons and three daughters. The one Luther loved most was Magdalena, the saintly little creature who died in his arms at the age of fourteen and is the subject of an appealing portrait by one of the Cranach school.

During the early years of Luther's married life, the affairs of the great world pressed with growing weight upon him and his associates. The family living-room at the Black Cloister was littered with books and papers, constantly filled by people in trouble, messengers, refugees, negotiators and officials. In the period following the Peasants' Revolt, the content of the German crisis became political rather than social, yet it remained equally relevant to the fate of Luther's movement. At the Diet of Speyer in August 1526 the Catholics still preserved their majority, except among the delegates of the Imperial cities, yet they had no desire to plunge the Empire into civil war in order to enforce the Edict of Worms. On their side the Protestant powers remained most reluctant to divide the Empire on the basis of a religious rift which few if any conceived to be permanent. Compromise and procrastination ensued. It was agreed that the Edict could not yet everywhere be executed, and that meanwhile the states would act 'in such a manner as all trusted to justify before God and the Imperial Majesty'. The Emperor viewed this not as a license for Lutheranism but merely as a truce accepted until a General Council of the Church should provide ecclesiastical reform and final settlement. To us the arrangement dimly heralds the coming triumph of the principle *cujus regio, ejus religio*.

Two days after the Diet dispersed there occurred the disaster of Mohács, which drew King Ferdinand off toward the Magyar-Turkish whirlpool. About the same time Charles himself was losing control over Rome. The evasive Medici Pope Clement VII became ever more closely bound to Francis I and so entered the path which led to the running amok of the Imperial armies and, in May 1527, to the appalling sack of Rome at their hands. These circumstances not only prevented papal-imperial reforms in Germany but removed barriers to the extension and consolidation of Lutheranism. The year 1528 saw Philip of Hesse acting under the influence of the adventurer Otto von Pack, who persuaded him that a great Catholic alliance had been secretly formed to crush the Protestant princes. Philip hence formed a rival alliance in order to wage a preventive war, and he was with difficulty dissuaded by John of Saxony and other moderates from attacking the prince-bishoprics along the Main. But by this time the Pope had been dragged back into subjection and Ferdinand could take a further initiative. At Speyer in April 1529 he induced a majority of the Diet to annul the resolutions of 1526, to decree that religious changes must cease, and to demand that episcopal jurisdiction be restored in those states where it had been abolished. Faced by these pressures, the Lutheran members presented their official 'Protestation', from which the term 'Protestant' derived: ever since then this negative term has been a handicap to a movement never in fact lacking positive emphases. The Protestation was signed by the Elector of Saxony, Landgrave Philip, Margrave George of Ansbach, Prince Wolfgang of Anhalt, a representative of the Duke of Brunswick-Lüneburg and some fourteen cities, led by Strassburg, Nuremberg, Ulm and Constance. The cities, most of which lay near or surrounded by Catholic states, ran the chief risks by this act of defiance.

Early in October 1529 Philip of Hesse succeeded in bringing together Luther and Zwingli at his castle overlooking the city of Marburg. The Landgrave and the Zürich Reformers conceived of a vast Protestant union stretching from Switzerland to Denmark; with the inevitable French backing, this might once for all cripple the Habsburgs. The events of that summer had made such a union doubly desirable, for they had included a close *rapprochement* between Charles and Pope Clement, and a treaty between the former and Francis at Cambrai. On the other hand, theological differences presented the Protestant groups with difficulties greater than those arising in the field of secular diplomacy. The clash that developed at Marburg over the doctrine of the Lord's Supper might well have been anticipated, since as early as 1525 Zwingli's tract *On the True and False Religion* had condemned Luther's eucharistic doctrine. There had succeeded a controversy between Oecolampadius, championing the Swiss symbolic memorial-service, and Johannes Brenz, the Swabian who became one of the stoutest pillars of Lutheran theology. In writing several of his sermons and tracts between 1526 and 1528, Luther had clarified his own mind on the nature of the Presence, and the Marburg meeting found him committed and unreceptive. These writings had culminated in *A Confession on the Lord's Supper*, in which he remarks that 'one should avoid Zwingli and his books as devilish poison of Satan'. Yet this book convinced Martin Bucer that Luther did not in fact maintain a corporeal Presence in the sacrament, and so Bucer came to Marburg prepared to mediate between the two parties. There his position was uncomfortable, for in Luther's eyes he had misrepresented and criticised Lutheran views in his recent writings.

For the initial Marburg discussions Landgrave Philip paired off Luther with Oecolampadius and Melanchthon with Zwingli, thus avoiding an early clash between the two most obstinate champions. These private conversations proceeded quietly, but the opening of the formal session began with Luther's famous gesture, the chalking of the words *hoc est corpus meum* on the table. From the first he blandly assumed that the whole burden of proof lay with those who challenged his own literal interpre-

tation of these words. Again, as shown by a letter of Melanchthon written during the first days, the Lutherans thought of
Zwingli as an ill-equipped theologian. After long and technical
discussions concerning the location of the risen Christ, it became clear that while the Zwinglians did acknowledge a spiritual communion between Christ and the devout communicant,
they would travel no further than this in Luther's direction.
Though the parties swiftly reached agreement on fourteen other
theological issues, this failure to agree over the nature of the
eucharist had great historical significance. It meant that Luther
failed to absorb the Swiss, that the Swiss Reformation would
maintain its separate identity, that in the end, thanks largely to
Calvin's influence, the majority of Protestants throughout the
world would not be members of Lutheran churches. Marburg
was a monument to the non-political nature of Luther and
Lutheranism. The final outcome he could not have foreseen,
but even had he done so, it would have made no difference to
his stand. On one or two occasions in his career Luther may
have listened to the voice of expediency, but it was never in
relation to a matter of this magnitude. As for Zwingli, he withdrew from the conference far more emotionally affected by
failure than Luther. He went home to stumble through the last
act of his personal tragedy and two years later he died at
Kappel in heroic conflict with the Catholic Forest Cantons.
Luther, sad to record, heard of his death with relief rather than
regret.

Soon after Marburg matters began to move again upon the
German political front. The Emperor's return was followed in
June 1530 by the Diet of Augsburg. Though he was accompanied by the papal nuncio Campeggio, Charles adopted an
impartial demeanour and encouraged people to regard him as
a *deus ex machina*, coming to judge all parties from his high
throne. Since Luther still lay under the ban of the Empire, he
could not attend the Diet but took up his position at Coburg
on the southern extremity of the Saxon lands, whence he could
maintain touch with the official delegation headed by Melanchthon. The latter has all too often been charged with adopting
servile attitudes at Augsburg. Fearful of civil war, troubled by

his sense of the corruption and ignorance besetting a divided land, more at ease with scholars than with potentates, Philip seems to cut an unheroic figure. Yet the positive aspects of his mind and his mission should not be overlooked. A truly ecumenical thinker, he sought not to issue further defiant manifestos but to foster the cause of reunion, to stress the continuity of Lutheran teaching from that of the Catholic Church. It was scarcely his fault if most of the Catholic princes and papal diplomats took moderation for weakness and became less inclined than ever to envisage any sort of concessions. Yet just as the intransigent Luther had failed to unite Protestantism, so now the intransigent Catholics failed to divide Lutheranism. When they refused to discuss communion in both kinds and clerical marriage, even Melanchthon could negotiate no further, and the Lutheran movement fell back more securely into Luther's waiting hands.

The permanent result of Melanchthon's mildness was the saddling of the Lutheran establishment with the Confession of Augsburg, drawn up on this occasion by him, Spalatin and others with some uneasy criticism from Luther in the background. Philip's detractors have called it a timid diplomatic document, while his admirers have claimed that, for all its gentleness, it sacrifices no essentials of the Evangelical faith. For good or ill it gained henceforth a high place among the foundation-charters of the Lutheran Church. It condemned the sectarians and Zwinglians, but it made no attack on the papal supremacy, on purgatory and indulgences, on the non-Scriptural sacraments. If it argued the need to accord the communion-cup to the laity and marriage to the clergy, it spoke of the eucharist in terms so vague as to be almost acceptable to Catholics. Though its phraseology on justification by faith was firm enough, it made no reference to the priesthood of all believers. From the Pope's standpoint, its most dangerous feature was an appeal to the decisions of a future General Council. At the Diet Charles heard this document read, but he then threatened the Lutherans with action if they refused to return to the fold. Philip of Hesse rode away without taking leave of the Emperor, and though the other Protestant princes avoided this incivility, they nevertheless stood firm. So did the perilously-placed cities, despite the heavier pressures brought to bear on them after the princes had left the Diet. Augsburg itself, the Emperor within its walls and Bavaria at its gates, refused to promise compliance. The four cities of Strassburg, Constance, Lindau and Memmingen signed the *Confessio Tetrapolitana*, drawn up by Bucer and distinctly more radical than that of Augsburg.

When at last the Protestant members had gone, the Catholics agreed upon the final Recess, which returned to the position at Worms nine years earlier. It condemned the Lutherans equally with the Zwinglians and sectarians; it demanded the return of sequestrated church properties, the punishment of married clergy, a strict censorship over preaching and publication. Even so, it proved a pious declaration rather than a trumpet-call to crusade. At the Diet itself Charles had found the Catholic princes more than reluctant to put forces into his hands; they felt that the sequel to his armed victory over the heretics might prove almost as dangerous to themselves as to their Protestant fellows. Throughout this period none of the princes feared more for their *Libertät* (i.e. privileges) than did the rulers of the most strongly Catholic territory: the Wittelsbach Dukes of Bavaria, whose old enmity with Austria was complicated by desire for a crown of their own. Hence the Diet of Augsburg decided in effect to leave crusading to the Catholic leaders most distracted by rival dangers and responsibilities: the Emperor Charles and his brother Ferdinand. Accordingly, while Luther's early career must be seen against the background of abortive social revolution, his later career continued against one of political stalemate.

After the Diet Luther's profound scruples against armed opposition to the Emperor were partially overcome by the arguments of his more militant supporters, while by a personal visit to Coburg Martin Bucer did much to allay his resentment against Strassburg and the semi-Zwinglian Protestants of south-western Germany. These two developments opened the way toward the League of Schmalkalden, concluded in February 1531 by six princes and ten cities. A constitution with provision both for legal and for military resistance was established in 1532 and subsequently revised. Before Luther's death almost all the German Protestant states large and small had joined this league. While the Swiss avoided a direct attachment, Strassburg and the south-western cities played their usual intermediary part and had an understanding with Hesse on the one hand and with Zürich on the other. Yet the defeat and death of Zwingli caused the Strassburgers and their allies to look increasingly to their north and to take ever more seriously the doctrinal claims of Wittenberg.

While this formidable alliance was building, the Emperor's opportunities for a counterstroke did not greatly improve. In 1531 he succeeded in bribing all the Electors except John of Saxony to confer on his brother the title of King of the Romans, and thereby to recognise Ferdinand as his successor on the Imperial throne. On the other hand the Turks remained aggressive, the Popes unreliable, King Francis ever ready to intrigue with the Turks or adopt the cause of any refractory German prince. In the summer of 1532 Charles felt bound to accept a truce at Nuremberg, whereby he undertook to suspend legal proceedings against the Lutheran allies pending the deliberation of a General Council or, in default of such, to those of a future Diet. For their part the Protestants demonstrated their loyalty to the Empire by despatching against the Turks more than the number of troops due from them.

The Peace of Nuremberg did not, however, prevent Philip of Hesse from re-arming with the aid of French money: in 1534 it did not prevent him from restoring by force the Protestant Duke Ulrich of Württemberg, whose territory had been seized some fifteen years earlier by the Swabian League and put under Habsburg administration. This dramatic restoration not only drove another Protestant wedge into southern Germany, but occasioned the dissolution of the Swabian League itself. Hitherto a tool of Habsburg policy, and the mainstay of order in southern Germany, it had already been weakened by the secession of many Protestant cities. Duke Ulrich himself leaned to Zwinglianism and at first set up a church with features drawn both from Wittenberg and from Zürich. But subsequently the Duchy became a wholly Lutheran state and a great rallying point for southern Protestantism. At Tübingen in 1536 Duke Ulrich founded the Protestant seminary in the former Augustinian house, while at Freudenstadt in the Black Forest we may still admire the geometrical town-planning of a later Duke of Württemberg, who founded the place in 1599 as a model settlement for the Protestant refugees flooding into his dominions from the Habsburg lands.

Despite Philip's success, the majority of the Lutheran princes and cities shared Luther's distrust for foreign powers and his lingering regard for the Emperor. The Reformation elucidates the strength as well as the weakness of Imperial loyalties, and though Charles with his international interests was a far from ideal German Emperor, thoughtful Germans could now in 1535 compare two spectacles: that of Charles fighting the infidel in Tunisia with that of Francis, in cynical league with the Grand Turk.

These years 1528-35 were possibly the period of most rapid expansion for Lutheranism, though later on, despite the sensational reverses of 1546-7, it was to retain a good deal of its religious momentum until around 1560. We can hardly compile neat diagrams or maps of the expansion, since in states like Mecklenburg and cities like Hamburg the transition was managed very gradually. In the great province of Silesia, where even the Bishop of Breslau had studied under Luther and Melanchthon, some of the principalities, duchies and counties had fully accepted the Reformation by 1534, while in others Habsburg influence was able to resist the demands of the gentry and the estates for a further decade. Conversely the religious movement could persist for decades in territories under Catholic rulers. Even in the early days it was very far from being limited to north Germany and Scandinavia. Between 1520 and 1560, the university of Wittenberg, the main generator of the religious movement and the trainer of its devoted missionaries, admitted some 16,000 students. The admission-registers show that while about a third of these came from north Germany, another third were attracted from south Germany and the rest from foreign lands. While the governments of Austria, Bavaria and the southern prince-bishoprics ostensibly stood firm, they failed to check Protestant infiltration of their own territories, let alone to forestall the Württemberg *coup* of 1534. Most of the leading Swabian cities were Protestant by 1528. In that same year, a church-visitation of the Habsburg duchy of Styria shows that several towns and many of the nobles had already changed their religious allegiances.

Nevertheless the missionaries met a readier response from people and politicians who did not have to live closely alongside the Habsburgs, the Wittelsbachs and the prince-bishops. The solid core of Lutheranism hence lay in the north. By 1529 the reform of Brunswick-Lüneburg and Goslar had been completed; so had that of the great Hanseatic cities of Bremen and Hamburg. By 1530–31 the Baltic associates and neighbours of the latter had followed: Lübeck, Rostock, Wismar and Greifswald. Dominance over the southern Baltic coast came to completion during the thirties with the adhesion of Pomerania and Mecklenburg, and with the establishment of Lutheran churches in Schleswig and Holstein under the direction of their overlords the Danish kings. The latter were closely advised by Johann Bugenhagen, the Pomeranian divine intimately associated with Luther at Wittenburg and serving as his chief ambassador to foreign states. From the accession of Elector Joachim II in 1535 Brandenburg allowed Lutheran preachers, but it was the pressure of the cities and the estates that four years later induced the conciliatory Elector to make Lutheranism the state-religion. The Baltic littoral and Brandenburg remained free from Austro-Bavarian military pressures for a century. Then the great menace by Ferdinand II and Wallenstein was soon dispersed by the mighty counterstroke of their protector Gustavus Adolphus of Sweden.

The other princes and princelings of northern Germany gradually entered the Lutheran fold as the complexities of self-interest and religious conviction appealed to their minds. The Counts of Mansfield, under whom Luther was born and died, took the step in 1529. The bishoprics of Lübeck, Schwerin, Brandenburg and Schleswig—to mention only the larger ones— followed Prussia along the path of Protestant secularisation. The threats made by Duke Henry of Brunswick-Wolfenbüttel against the cities of Brunswick and Goslar gave John Frederick of Saxony and Philip of Hesse the excuse to drive him from his territories, and the Brunswick states then adhered in a piece-meal fashion. The Archbishop of Mainz lost control of Magde-burg and Halberstadt, though their conversion was not officially recognised for a couple of decades. As Ernestine Saxony had been the first major northern state to accept Lutheran prin-ciples, so Albertine Saxony was the last, for until his death in the spring of 1539 Duke George looked coldly upon the Evan-gelical enthusiasm of his cousins and criticised Luther with unabated bitterness. Even on his death, a strong conservative party, anxious to prevent the acquisition of church-properties by their ruler, opposed the Protestant designs of his brother and successor Henry II. In 1541 Henry's death made way for the young and vigorous Duke Maurice, the architect of a local Reformation which did not lack a measure of social idealism. A sizeable proportion of the proceeds of the monastic lands went to endow the university of Leipzig and to found three impor-tant schools at Meissen, Merseburg and Schulpforte. In the case of Albertine Saxony as in those of Württemberg and Hesse, it may clearly be shown that the spoils of the Reformation did not merely go into the private coffers of the princes, but in large part served public purposes, including education and charity.

Though the various rulers gained in prestige, their wealth and their material power did not in fact benefit greatly from the Reformation, for everywhere their Estates saw to it that they received as little as possible. Within a few years the rise of prices ensured that princely governments became more de-pendent than ever upon the money-grants of Estates. On the other hand, it seems equally clear that many of the noble families in the Lutheran states benefited from their purchases of former monastic lands. By this time extremely interested in the high profits accruing from grain and other food-stuffs, the north German Junkers accomplished for their own private profit the rehabilitation of agriculture which Luther had de-sired on social grounds. As a class they prospered faster than the towns, while their monopoly of government offices and their predominance in the various Estates increased their political weight *pari passu* with their wealth. This process was perhaps most marked in Prussia, Brandenburg and Pomerania, where the rulers were forced by lack of money to sell or pawn ex-monastic estates to the wealthier nobles. It was not until the mid-seventeenth century that the Hohenzollerns, having united these great provinces under a single ruler, built up their power to the point where they stood in real partnership with their nobility.

It seems unlikely that the secularisation of church lands played a major part in depressing the living-standards and the legal status of the peasantry. Those very secular-minded aristocrats, the ecclesiastical landlords, were among the most oppressive and least popular in Germany; one may hardly suppose that their survival in greater numbers would have helped the unprivileged classes. In many parts of central and eastern Europe the status of the peasantry declined during the century following the Reformation. Yet this process was far from being limited to Protestant countries, where lay landlords replaced monasteries. It was due in the main to the very high profits now accruing to all landowners who could increase labour-services and extend their demesne-farming by evicting or buying out their peasant-farmers.

In north-western Germany as in the south, the new faith spread spontaneously even into those areas where governments were hostile or apathetic. After the example of Prussia, several of the prince-bishops secularised their states. At Cologne, hitherto a focus of conservatism, the Elector Hermann von Wied relinquished his former hostility and in 1536 began to introduce semi-Protestant liturgical changes. Three years later he was consulting Melanchthon and Bucer; his gradual transfer from Catholic reform to Protestantism ultimately caused Paul III to decree his excommunication. Of all the German princes, Archbishop Hermann attained the closest connection with our English Reformation, since the liturgy he sponsored in the so-called *Consultatio* of 1543 appeared in English translation five years later, and it influenced Archbishop Cranmer as he compiled the first Anglican *Book of Common Prayer* (1549).

In earlier years Hermann von Wied had stood among the active opponents of Anabaptism, which from its new seed-bed in the Netherlands spread outward both into the Rhineland and into Westphalia. In the latter region, where the chief ruler was the libertine bishop of Münster Franz von Waldeck, the Catholics made no effective resistance to the new movements, and by the early thirties many towns had accepted Protestantism. Then in 1534–5 came a most unexpected event. The city of Münster itself fell under the control of an Anabaptist group, led by Netherlandish followers of the fanatical Melchior Hoffmann. There followed the establishment of the Kingdom of the Saints under the local cloth-merchant Bernhard Knipperdolling and the two Dutch prophets Jan Matthys and Jan Beukels, *alias* John of Leyden. Finally in July 1535 the prince-bishop, aided by Lutheran as well as by Catholic rulers, recaptured the city and slew most of the defenders.

The repercussions of this lurid affair proved endless. The social significance of Münster Anabaptism—which introduced communism and polygamy only under the desperate stresses of a long siege—has doubtless been exaggerated from that day to this. The episode was not typical of Anabaptism, yet it did great harm not only to that movement but to Protestantism as a whole. Not merely did it tarnish the Reformation in Catholic and non-committed opinion; more significantly, it encouraged the illiberal tendencies of both Lutherans and Zwinglians, driving them into fresh displays of conservatism calculated to dissociate them from the Münster fanatics and convince the world of their respectability. Heinrich Bullinger, Zwingli's statesmanlike successor at Zürich, wrote the most famous of the attacks upon Anabaptism, while the Lutherans themselves were further discouraged from stressing either Christian liberty or the congregationalist elements apparent in Gospel Christianity. Everywhere the poor, heroic Anabaptists were burned and drowned by Catholic authorities and on a lesser scale by Protestants. It seems indeed one of the sadder ironies of religious history that this hardening among 'orthodox' Protestants came at the moment when Anabaptist extremism was making its exit. From around the time of Münster the movement as a whole was rejecting the notion of a Kingdom of the Saints based upon the sword. Its chief leader was now Menno Simons, who, counselling passive resistance and willingness to undergo martyrdom, pieced together the broken fragments of the movement and preserved the more valuable elements in its teaching.

We have already described Luther's rousing appeal of 1520 for the freedom of the Christian conscience. At that time he had seen himself as the deliverer of Christians from laws fabricated by Rome without scriptural warrant. Even then he can hardly have wanted to sanction the vagaries and enthusiasms attendant upon complete freedom of religious expression, but his belief in the irresistible Word appears to have included a confident hope that the nation would spontaneously rally round his banner and substitute an agreed discipline based on the Scriptures for the man-made laws he was denouncing. And though soon afterwards he encountered the sectarians, he maintained his liberal attitude in the tract *Of Secular Authority* published in 1523. Here faith is still regarded as a free action to which no man can be forced; Augustine is cited to the effect that Christ wants only a free and willing obedience. As for heresy, it is a spiritual thing and cannot be struck down by mere material weapons. Around this time, however, Luther's impulsive declarations cannot be harmonised. While in 1524 he urged that sectarians, even Anabaptists, should be allowed freedom to preach and to 'fall upon one another and fight it out', in the previous year he had called the Catholic mass a public blasphemy, to be put down by public authority. His own Elector reproved him for these inconsistent utterances and urged him to practise what he preached.

Then came the disorders of 1524–5, followed by the heavy responsibility to establish and defend the Evangelical churches in Saxony and elsewhere. It now seemed that in his inscrutable wisdom God was not granting a swift victory; that the Word had not after all suddenly prompted the whole nation to accept the message entrusted to Luther. Without openly abandoning his doctrine of the free conscience, the latter now began to stress the responsibility of the civil State both to suppress the 'abomination' of the mass and to prohibit sectarian preaching. Refusal by Catholics or sectarians to listen to instruction he now regarded as almost criminal perversity. In 1529 he upheld the right of the prince to compel people to attend sermons, if only to learn their ethical duties. In 1530–31, some years before Münster, he and Melanchthon sanctioned the harshest penalties against the Anabaptists. In 1532 he encouraged Duke Albert of Prussia to expel even Zwinglians from Prussian territory, on the ground that their eucharistic views denied a vital part of the faith agreed for 1500 years. Thus within a decade the glorious assertions of 1520 had come to mean very little in terms of actual freedom throughout the Lutheran lands. In fairness to Luther certain extenuating points might be made. His withdrawal from practical toleration was in large part based on secular fears shared by the great majority of his contemporaries. 'A secular prince', he wrote in 1526, 'should ensure that his subjects are not led into strife by rival preachers, whence factions and disturbances might arise, but in any one place there should be only one kind of preaching.' This fear, the parent of *cujus regio, ejus religio*, he frequently reiterated. Anabaptists apart, Luther abhorred the death-penalty for religious opinions and denounced it in the most moving terms. The states guided by him were certainly among the least cruel persecutors of sixteenth-century Europe; banishment was harsh, but far less harsh than the mass burnings and drownings practised in the Netherlands and elsewhere. In assessing tolerance, attention must be paid to actions as well as to theory.

As the various German princes, city councillors and pastors faced the problems involved in the establishment of Lutheran churches, they found useful guidance in the methods already tested in Electoral Saxony. Despite his distrust of political influences upon church government, Luther now felt himself forced to collaborate with lay officialdom in planning and executing measures of reform. To this course he was impelled by his awareness that the fate of his cause depended upon its ability to create an able and dedicated pastorate. Under his guidance a general visitation of churches and clergy in Electoral Saxony was prepared and carried through in 1527–8. Five regional commissions appointed by the Elector, each consisting of professors, court officials and prominent divines, were provided with elaborate instructions and allowed to inspect, to report and to reform. They found much indifference and ignorance even among clerics who nominally accepted the Reformation. Already low in the preceding years, standards seemed to have sunk still further during the time of confusion before and after the Peasants' Revolt. Some ministers could not repeat the Ten Commandments or the Lord's Prayer; others were notorious brewers, drinkers and gamesters; many still lived in concubinage. Removing the grosser misfits, the commissioners urged the remainder to study the catechisms which Luther prepared especially for the purpose. The commissioners were at first instructed to exercise patience with clerics who had recently left the Roman allegiance, but during the thirties a stricter discipline was imposed both in Saxony and in those many other Lutheran states which accepted the Saxon patterns. Superintendents or boards were now despatched to conduct elaborate examinations of candidates for the ministry.

Besides his longer and shorter catechisms, Luther prepared great numbers of brief sermons: the immensely influential *Kirchenpostillen*, which the less educated clergy could memorise or even read out from their pulpits. During the early years such help proved most necessary, since the lack of university-trained pastors forced the authorities to appoint many emergency preachers (*Notprediger*) with little Latin or theology. As late as 1539 these humble clerics numbered a third of the ordinations held at Wittenberg, but then the figure sank to one-sixth by 1546 and soon afterwards virtually to nil. Steps were taken to allow the pastors some authority over their flocks; they were permitted, after giving repeated brotherly warnings, to place serious sinners under the minor excommunication, which debarred from communion but allowed attendance at sermons, so as to afford a better chance of amendment. Luther had no desire whatever to re-establish anything like the old system of canon law, but some provision had to be made for cases involving marriage, divorce, inheritance and other matters hitherto reserved to the ecclesiastical courts. In 1539 the Elector

John Frederick did in fact establish a consistory court at Wittenberg to exercise these branches of jurisdiction.

Amid these steps to instruct and strengthen the clergy, Luther's basic position on the priesthood of all Christians was by no means abandoned: the pastor did not belong to a separate hierarchy, endowed with special privileges and sacramental functions. He was the spiritual leader of his congregation, but at the same time responsible to this partially self-governing body. Luther and his associates had also to educate congregations in their new duties. In particular they had to be induced to provide financial maintenance for their clergy, many of whom were at first compelled to practise trades on weekdays in order to eke out their shrunken emoluments. Through the Elector and the visitors Luther managed to establish a small tax, the *Beichtpfennig* or communion penny, paid four times a year by all parishioners over the age of twelve. Even so, an adequate system of remuneration was scarcely attained until after his death. In the meantime there were wide differences between the poor country pastors and their eminent city colleagues: Bugenhagen at Wittenberg, Amsdorf at Magdeburg, Jonas at Halle and Brenz at Schwäbisch Hall, men with good salaries, fine libraries and a high status in society. But these pillars of the new church earned their privileges. Though they were helped by assistants, they lived laborious lives, preaching vast numbers of sermons, catechising the young, visiting the sick, going off on missions and deputations, or to act as advisers on the problems of newly-won territories.

The Protestant Reformation and the Catholic Counter-Reformation both achieved great successes by offering new standards to the parochial clergy, toward whose formation and guidance the medieval church had contributed so meagerly. Luther deserves no small share of the credit for these honest and ultimately successful endeavours. Despite his natural lack of discretion and his irascibility, he made a better ecclesiastical administrator than might have been anticipated. He could supply what every new system needs: drive and resolution rather than meticulous adherence to formulae. During his later years Luther was surrounded by able but rather ordinary minds, supplementing his deficiencies, revering his spiritual authority, yet preparing even before he was gone to reduce his inspirations to new clerical codes. This should occasion us no surprise, for has it not been the common fate of all prophets and renovators in Christian history?

We have already hinted at some of the theories of Church, State and society upon which Luther based his reforms. He developed these theories as corollaries to his 'new' theology of 1518–19, yet only by gradual and complex stages did he emancipate himself from the traditional concepts expressed in his earlier writings. In Luther's thought we have sometimes to deal with outright inconsistencies: far more significantly, we have to reckon with growth and development, with agonising reappraisals spread across laborious years. New and original systems of thought seldom leap fully armed from the heads of their authors. Luther's maturer views on these important matters take shape throughout numerous sermons and tracts of the twenties and thirties; on Church and State he makes notable advances through the tractates *Of Secular Authority* (1523), *The Bondage of the Will* (1525), *Can Soldiers be Christians?* (1526) and in the sermons on St. Matthew published in 1532.

Like the Catholic writers, he often speaks of the Church as the 'mystical body of Christ', but whereas they tended primarily to see this body in a priestly hierarchy administering the sacraments, Luther saw it as a community of equal Christian believers called together and constituted by the Word. With him this fellowship becomes primary, not secondary.

> The consequence of being one with Christ is that we are one also among ourselves. . . . As the grains of corn are milled they are blended with one another. None of it keeps its own flour, but it is mixed with that of others and is made part of it. . . . [So also among Christians] none is for himself, but everyone shows and spreads himself among his fellows in love.

Luther's view of the Church was eminently non-sectarian, despite his belief that real Christians were in a minority. He believed that every man, woman and child should be admitted to church membership and so exposed to the enlightenment of the Word. He wanted to find a middle path between the forcing of consciences and a chaos of autonomous congregations or rival churches. While he maintained the right of a congregation to approve its own ministers, to manage its own social and educational work, even to regulate details of worship, he tended in practice to equate congregations with civil communities, for whom rulers and magistrates would normally speak.

Luther interpreted the Scriptures to mean that both the individual Christian and the Church itself exist simultaneously in two separate realms of being: before the throne of God, and here in a confused and sinful world. In the higher realm, where man's salvation is transacted, God rules alone and man has no effective free-will. In the realm of the world and of civil justice, God rules indirectly through human reason and statesmanship, while man does exercise free-will. So too with the Church: a spiritual Church exists in the higher realm, but the organisation of the Church on earth is merely a part of God's world-government, controlled by reason. The two realms cannot be 'mixed' here on earth, as the sectarians desire. Again, God has commissioned no religious mediators to stand between himself and the rest of mankind; no hierarchy, clerical or lay, has been entrusted to wield a divine jurisdiction over things of the spirit.

In his earlier works Luther accepts the secular State as a harsh bridle fastened by God upon the unruly and the wicked, but having little relevance to Christians, who live by the law of love. Later on, he tends to give a somewhat more positive value to worldly government, which he now sees not merely as checking the wicked but as ordained by God to govern both the wicked and the Christians alike in the affairs of this world. Nevertheless, even in his later writings Luther sharply restricts the State to its own sphere: this evil and ephemeral secular life. His State is anything but a 'Christian State', entitled to govern the inner life and the consciences of men. Even in the person of a ruler, there are two quite distinct functions: that of Christian, and that of ruler.

Every Christian must be some sort of worldly person, since he is at least in body and goods subject to the Emperor. But for his own person in his Christian life, he is all alone under Christ. . . . A prince can surely be a Christian, but as a Christian he cannot rule. . . . The person is surely a Christian, but the office of prince has nothing to do with his Christianity.

We on earth must give Caesar what is Caesar's, but as Christians

we are already placed in another higher existence, which is a divine eternal kingdom, where one needs none of the things that belong to the world, but every one of us is for himself in Christ a lord both over the Devil and over the whole world.

If princes and magistrates assume any form of ecclesiastical leadership, they should do so as eminent members of the congregation, not by virtue of their civil offices. Here, however, the hard facts soon outran Luther's theoretical distinctions. Commissioners and superintendents appointed by princes looked uncommonly like state-officials controlling the life of the Church. Whatever his personal ideals, Luther in effect did much to establish the *Landeskirche*, the territorial church comprising the whole population of a state, subject to various forms of princely or civic control, affording little initiative to individuals or local congregations, having its ecclesiastical discipline, its church schools, and even in limited degree its worship regulated or supervised by commissions.

Such elements in Lutheranism can, of course, easily be exaggerated, not least by those unaware of the immense powers exerted by medieval kings over their national churches. The Lutheran lay authorities did not devise or significantly change the essentials of belief and devotion. These essentials came from Luther and the divines. Yet that this relationship tended to glorify the German princes in the eyes of their subjects cannot be denied, and it may be placed among the many factors which in more recent times hampered the rise of critical minds and democratic initiatives in German society. On the other hand, the fantasy that holds Luther responsible for Prussian state-worship and even for National Socialism is to be deplored. He would have been horrified by some features of the former and by everything about the latter. In Luther's day the apotheosis of princes had arisen in many parts of Europe, not least in the England of Henry VIII. And we have only to remember the Valois, the Bourbons, the Habsburgs and the Wittelsbachs to realise that the chief trend-setters of absolutism were—and were long to remain—Catholic and not Lutheran rulers. The Great Elector, the architect of modern autocracy in Brandenburg-Prussia, was a Calvinist. Even in Prussia the hard facts of geography were the main promoters of militarist centralisation; Lutheranism had little to do with the personality or policies of Frederick the Great. In short, he inherited the drift to autocracy; he can have made no significant contribution to so broad a trend; he could not even have foreseen the whole of that great complex of causes which gave birth to the various absolutist states. From his day to ours the latter have been largely the offspring of secular factors and worldly leaders. Furthermore, for a century or so after Luther's death the political influence of Lutheranism appears on the whole beneficent. The German Lutheran states were the least aggressive in Europe. While their rulers present a highly mixed spectacle, several of them like August I of Saxony, William IV of Hesse-Cassel, John George of Brandenburg and Christoph of Württemberg, exemplify the paternal rule of that age at its very best. Such were the enlightened autocrats of their day, and in those hard times men were fortunate to be the subjects of a genuine godly prince.

One of the most effective of Luther's personal contributions to the Evangelical Church lay in the liturgical and musical fields. His *Formula Missae* of 1523 remained in Latin; apart from the excision of the canon (the long consecratory prayer stressing the sacrificial aspect of the mass) it represented a very conservative revision. Thomas Müntzer had already prepared a German mass which Luther admired until he discovered the identity of the author. While never guilty of linguistic fanaticism, he soon came to see the logic of a step which brought a detailed understanding of the service within the reach of ordinary people. In 1526 he produced his own vernacular mass, which soon became the common property of the emergent Lutheran world. An enthusiastic and competent musician from early days, he then set about reforming the musical elements of the liturgy: the passages intoned by the pastor, the chorales sung by the choir, the congregational hymns. As always, he put religious understanding first, insisting that every word should be audible, one note used for one syllable. He demanded organ accompaniments which avoided drowning the words; he forbade settings which involved arbitrary rearrangement of the scriptural texts, for example conflations of the four Gospels. As a consequence of this tradition, Bach had therefore to write a *St. Matthew Passion* or a *St. John Passion*, but not an amalgam of the two. But with these safeguards Luther sought to use all the contemporary resources of music to bring out the emotions and moods of the text. Showing here a remarkable freedom from confessional prejudices, he loved the polyphonic chorales of the late medieval Netherlandish school, incorporated them into the life of his own churches and urged the princes to employ professional choirs capable of tackling such works. It was of this music that he wrote:

> One perceives with astonishment the grand and perfect wisdom of God in his marvellous work of music, where one voice takes a simple part, while around it sing three, four or five other voices, leaping about, wonderfully enhancing the simple part, like a dance in heaven . . . he who does not find this an inexpressible miracle of the Lord is in truth a blockhead and unworthy to be considered a man.

On the other hand, Lutheran notions of worship involved congregational participation on a scale unknown in pre-Reformation times. Hence the writing and composition of hymns was recognised from the early days as a crucial task. Luther's first little book of *Geistliche Lieder* had only eight hymns, of which four were his own. Greatly enlarged editions soon followed and the last to leave his hands (1545) contained 129 items, the words of some 37 being commonly attributed to Luther. The degree of his own responsibility for the musical settings remains a matter for argument between the experts. His inspiration as a hymn-writer was again catholic and unprejudiced. He translated some old Latin hymns like Notke's *Media vita in morte sumus*; his famous *Aus tiefer Not* and *Ein' feste Burg* are both very free variations upon Psalms (cxxx and xlvi respectively), while he captured the spirit of German folksong in *Vom Himmel hoch da komm' ich her* and in *Ein Neues Lied wir heben an*. It should not, however, be supposed that this poetic side of early Lutheranism was a one-man enterprise. The movement enlisted a large number of skilful musicians, hymn-writers and didactic versifiers, of whom the most famous and prolific was Hans Sachs, the cobbler and *Meistersinger* of Nuremberg.

This side of Luther's work leads us into the imponderables of social and religious history, yet we may well conjecture that the enthusiasm and cohesion of the Lutheran congregations during the later sixteenth and seventeenth centuries owed at least as much to their musical life as to their rigid and dogmatic theological instruction. Certainly it is this that distinguished the Lutheran Church from the narrow and suspicious attitude of Calvinist puritanism, and it was among the uncovenanted mercies that the first major Protestant Church took its cue from the man who said:

> I have no use for cranks who despise music, because it is a gift of God. . . . Next after theology I give to music the highest place and the greatest honour . . . next to the Word of God only music deserves to be extolled as mistress and governess of the feelings of the human heart.

In another place, he praises music because it is non-polemical: it seems indeed a pleasant irony that this most polemical of men scored his least debatable triumph by inaugurating in so peaceable a spirit one of Europe's finest cultural traditions. By any standards this tradition would have been great, even had it not happened to culminate in the universal genius of Johann Sebastian Bach.

To understand the finer characteristics of Luther the man and the pastor we should no doubt turn aside from the spectacle of the earth-shaking Reformer to read the 3,000 or more extant letters and the other many evidences of his activity as a personal counsellor. They show beyond a doubt his ceaseless and truly helpful concern for the sick, the bereaved, the perplexed, the oppressed and persecuted, the sufferers from matrimonial problems. Everywhere he makes the Evangelical appeal to faith, yet over and above it he displays a rare human sympathy, an inspired common sense. Never, even to correspondents he has not met, is he the dry, impersonal confessor. During the bubonic plagues in Wittenberg he remains at his pastoral station: even when the university itself is evacuated he visits the sick and takes some of them into his house. No religious fatalist, he encourages everything that can be done by the medical treatment and precautions of the day. But of physical health in general he remarks that it "depends in large measure on the thoughts of our minds; this is in accord with the saying: *good cheer is half the battle.*"

Bitter experience makes him adjure depressed and tempted people to seek companionship, to go out and converse with anybody, above all to avoid those inventions of the Devil: fasting and solitude. He is forever pleading with authority on behalf of widows, orphans, impoverished students, refugees and prisoners. He believes in early marriage; he condemns parents who prevent it, or force unsuitable matches upon unwilling children. He strives to keep his students out of the disease-infested brothels; he castigates the sort of clericalism which disparages matrimony but allows adulterers and whores to enjoy high honour. His acceptance of the God-given origins of sex contrasts with the insensate legalism of a system that forced celibacy upon thousands of deluded people unfitted to embrace that way of life. To three nuns anxious to leave their convent and marry, he writes fearlessly in 1524:

Though women were ashamed to admit it, the Scriptures and our experience show that God gives only one person out of several thousand the gift to live chastely in a state of virginity. A woman does not have total mastery over herself: God so made her body that she should live with a man to bear and rear children. The words of *Genesis*, chapter I, clearly say this, and the parts of her body show sufficiently that God himself created her for this purpose. Just as eating, drinking, waking, and sleeping are appointed by God to be natural, so

God also makes it natural for a man and a woman to live together in marriage. This is enough, and no woman should be ashamed of the rôle for which God has created and fashioned her, and if she feels that she does not possess that exalted and rare gift (of celibacy), she may leave the convent and do what she is fitted by nature to do.

The next year Luther was similarly consulted by Wolfgang Reissenbusch, a former schoolmaster in a Saxon monastery, who hesitated to marry, even after his conversion to Protestantism, on account of an earlier vow. Luther reminded him that the prophets, the apostles and many early bishops and martyrs had not pretended to any superhuman contempt of marriage. "Adam's children are and remain men, and hence they should and must let men be begotten by them." Why should people be so stupid as to marvel when a man marries, when nobody marvels when he eats and drinks?

This is the Word of God, by whose power procreative seed is planted in man's body and a natural, ardent desire for woman is lit, and kept alight. This should not be restricted by vows or by laws, because it is God's law and doing. Let him who would live alone abandon the name of man and make himself an angel or a spirit . . . . Our bodies are largely the flesh of women, for by women we were conceived, given birth, suckled and nourished; so it is quite impossible to stay entirely apart from them. This is in accord with the Word of God.

And, one might add, this was an aspect of the Word seldom if ever proclaimed in such forthright accents amid the confused and stupid personal ethics of the middle ages and the earlier sixteenth century.

Chapter Six

Lutheranism Abroad

THE extension of Luther's teaching to the Scandinavian lands had profound effects upon their whole civilisation; conversely if less profoundly, Scandinavian Lutheranism did not fail to affect the course of German religious and political history. Quite apart from the remoteness of Rome and the in-adequacies of the late medieval Church in Scandinavia, the triumph of Lutheranism throughout this vast and sparsely-populated region seems largely due to three positive factors: the influence of the German trading colonies in all the northern cities; the ability and self-interest of Scandinavian kings; the enterprise and vigour of missionaries trained in Luther's circle. From Transylvania to London, from Bergen to Riga, the immediate enthusiasm of German expatriates for Luther's gospel contrasts with the initial coolness of its reception by the native populations. This popular and spontaneous movement through-out the German *diaspora* is yet one more of those features that belie the common image of Lutheranism as a creed imposed by wily German princes upon their ovine subjects. And to adapt a famous metaphor, Baltic Lutheranism found itself sitting crowned upon the graves of the Hanseatic League and the Teutonic Knights.

The speed of this northward thrust forms one of the most striking phenomena of the century. In Denmark the Reformation developed more swiftly than in some north German states. Herman Tast was preaching Lutheranism at Husum as early as 1522–3. In the latter year the monk Hans Tausen, having studied at Rostock, Copenhagen and Louvain, went on to Wittenberg, where he found inspiration in the lectures of Melanchthon. Having studied there for eighteen months, Tausen returned to his monastery, but by 1526 he was openly delivering Luther's message to enthusastic congregations at Viborg. Another visitor to Wittenberg in 1524 was the notorious King Christian II, whose reckless cruelty had marred his once promising championship of peasants and burghers and had led to his deposition the previous year. Having accepted the Reformation, Christian organised the translation and printing of the first Danish version of the New Testament. Sent at once into Denmark, this and subsequent editions greatly aided the work of the early missionaries. To these latter Christian's uncle and successor Frederick I allowed much freedom, and he soon announced that toleration would be accorded to their activities until a General Council should settle the faith. Both Frederick and a growing body of Danish aristocratic converts presented Lutheran divines to the parishes in their patronage, while by 1530 the King had begun to expropriate the monastic lands. The Carmelites, the most learned pre-Reformation religious order in Denmark, furnished at least seven of the leading native Lutheran pioneers. The death of Frederick I in 1533 was followed by a period of civil war over the succession, but by the summer of 1536 the victor was his son Christian III, who had long ago in the charge of his tutor actually attended the famous Diet of Worms and become a devotee of Luther. The following summer Christian III made a point of fetching the Pomeranian Bugenhagen from Wittenberg to crown him. *Pomeranus adhuc est in Dania*, wrote Luther in his friendly Latin, *et prosperantur omnia, quae Deus facit per eum. Regem coronavit et Reginam, quasi verus episcopus.*

The wars having left him deeply in debt, Christian secularised not only monastic lands but the temporalities of the higher clergy who had opposed him. He paid salaries to the new Lutheran bishops and maintained schools and hospitals formerly in ecclesiastical hands. Shortly after the coronation Bugenhagen ordained seven new superintendants or bishops of the Danish Church, and this action represented a break by Christian with the apostolic succession, which he could have preserved. Again with the aid of the Pomeranian, the King refounded the university of Copenhagen on a Protestant basis, envisaging it chiefly as a training school for clergy. His long and elaborate church ordinance of 1537 was supervised by Bugenhagen, while the revision of 1539 was referred to Luther himself before being submitted to the royal council and becoming the law of the Danish Church for a century and a half. The leading figure among the Evangelical bishops was Luther's own nominee Peder Palladius, who had studied for six years under Melanchthon. Almost all these Scandinavian leaders imitated their chief Saxon exemplar by becoming indefatigable writers. Along with Hans Tausen and the famous biblical translator and historian Christian Pedersen, Palladius gave the new Church an excellent literary basis as well as sound administrative foundations.

As early as 1526 a German ex-monk named Antonius had taught Lutheranism to the German colony in Bergen, but it was Palladius who began to convert the people of Norway, then a dependency of the Danish crown. Christian III extended his protection to the preachers, allowed the secularisation of church properties and roughly handled the Catholic prelates when they lent support to an invasion by the exiled Christian II. The defeat of this invasion meant the development of a Norwegian Reformation along Danish lines, and the foreign atmosphere—enhanced by the slowness of the Reformers to produce a Norse Bible—retarded its early advances among the common people, who were conservative without being ardently Catholic. In Norway, as in Denmark's lesser dependency Iceland, the secure establishment of a Lutheran Church belongs essentially to the second half of the century.

The Reformation in Sweden, likewise a lengthy process, was affected by political and social circumstances even more involved. Here serious resistance arose from the Catholic bishops led by Hans Brask of Linköping, and the political crisis ultimately took the form of a monarchical revolution. The claims of Christian II of Denmark extended also to Sweden, and the leader of the opposing Swedish national movement was that great dynastic founder Gustavus Vasa. When elected king in 1523, Gustavus together with his chancellor Archdeacon Laurentius Andreae favoured conservative and erastian reforms. Yet within a year or two Lutheran influences began to affect the

King and his circle. Meanwhile amongst the men of religion, the Swedish Reformation found its first patriarch in Olavus Petri, who had studied at Wittenberg from 1516 to 1518. If at the latter date his ideas were not fully abreast of Luther's, he had become a Lutheran by 1524, when as city clerk at Stockholm he began preaching to large congregations. In the following year Olavus set an example to the clergy by marrying; he also attracted the support of the German colony, then comprising a large part of the city's inhabitants. In 1526 he produced the first Swedish translation of the New Testament, having studied not only Luther's model but also the independent version of the Strassburg Reformers.

Pamphlets from all the main Protestant movements now flowed into Sweden, while Duke Albert of Prussia, who had signed an alliance with Gustavus, was not only despatching Protestant books but encouraging Gustavus to assume full control of the Swedish Church. In the summer of 1527 at the decisive Diet of Västerås Gustavus duly accomplished this feat by threatening abdication, by dividing the Catholic bishops and by appealing to the cupidity of the nobles. He was also aided by the good impression which the Lutheran preachers made upon the Estates. The Recess of Västerås transferred the 'surplus' revenues of bishops, chapters and monasteries to the Crown; in addition it permitted the nobility to recover from the religious houses all the land given them since the year 1454. It stipulated that 'God's Word might everywhere in the kingdom be purely preached'. The Diet also adopted the Västerås Ordinances, which destroyed the legal privileges of the clergy, curtailed their fees and fines, commanded that the Gospel be taught in every school and made competence to preach a necessary qualification for those ordained to the priesthood.

Though Catholic doctrine and the tie with Rome were not yet specifically abolished in Sweden, these changes gave full scope to the well-organised propaganda of the Reformers. While in many country districts traditional beliefs declined but slowly, the writings of Olavus Petri (chief among them his translation of Luther's sermons) dominated the book-market and consequently the minds of the growing literate population.

A series of liturgical reforms culminated in 1531 with a communion service in Swedish. In this same year Olavus' younger brother Laurentius Petri was appointed by the King as first Evangelical Archbishop, and another major personality entered the scene. Though trained at Wittenburg, Laurentius proved himself throughout the storms of the next four decades far more than a submissive royal agent. He saw that a mere state-Reformation under a despotic and moody king remained an inadequate foundation for the rebuilding of Christian life in Sweden. Illustrated more dramatically than in any German princedom, we observe here the extreme tension between Luther's principles, which assumed a considerable measure of ecclesiastical independence, and the grasping egotism of Renaissance statecraft. By 1539 the quarrel between Gustavus and his church-leaders became chronic. For a time the Archbishop was deprived of power in favour of the German superintendent Georg Norman, who ruthlessly stripped the churches of their treasures. Meanwhile the King sought to scare the opposition by sentences of death pronounced (though never executed) upon Olavus Petri and Laurentius Andreae.

In Sweden as in Germany and in England secular factions and the economic grievances of the common people gravely complicated the course of the Reformation. In 1530 the King demanded a tribute of one bell from every church, and in Bergslagen and Dalarna the men drove off his agents with sledge-hammers. The serious rebellions of 1542–3 in southern Sweden were sparked off by the royal demand for 'superfluous' church plate. While Swedish Catholicism was neither ardent nor well-informed, the priests could guide into religious channels the strong resentment aroused here in Småland and Blekinge by royal regulations hampering trade with Denmark. Though Gustavus crushed these risings, they helped to impress him with the need for moderation in his ecclesiastical policy. By 1544 he had restored the brothers Petri, yet he lost neither his suspicious attitude toward churchmen nor his urge to secularise church property. After the King's death in 1560, Archbishop Laurentius became better able to rationalise and even to liberalise the ordinances of the Swedish Lutheran Church. At the Synod of Uppsala in 1572 the normative function of the Bible was reasserted, Luther and Melanchthon both acknowledged as weighty though by no means final authorities, the schools firmly placed in the hands of the Church, the congregations given the right to elect their own pastors. From the material viewpoint the Swedish Reformation nevertheless provides an extreme example of erastianism; it has been calculated that the proportion of land held by the Church fell from 21% to nil, while that of the Crown increased from $5\frac{1}{2}$% to 28%. But the social, political and religious sequels can afford little comfort to economic determinists. The Crown did not achieve autocracy; the peasant-farmers did not lose their privileges; the Kings did not alter Lutheran doctrine.

In the northern kingdoms Lutheran devotional writings, biblical translations and liturgical works played a notable part in the emergence of their modern national literatures. In no mere narrowly doctrinal sense was Luther the step-father to these adolescent nations. Small in population, relatively simple in social structure, still acquiring a sense of national identity, and never deeply involved in Mediterranean traditions, the Scandinavian peoples were well adapted to receive the Evangelical religion and its broader concomitants. As an influence upon such national cultures, especially upon their literatures, Lutheranism found itself more powerful than did Anglicanism in England, a country about this time subjected to a greater complex of forces, both secular and religious. Most clearly of all did Lutheranism shape Finnish literature, which now began to exploit the extraordinary resources of a language wholly different from its teutonic and slavonic neighbours. That major Reformer Michael Agricola, who studied in Wittenberg from 1536 to 1539, is the acknowledged father of written Finnish, and he wrote as variously and as industriously as any of the Scandinavian divines. While his translation of the New Testament was not printed until 1548, Evangelical doctrines had in fact been preached at Turku over twenty years earlier and at Viipuri before 1530.

Over the waters and islands of the Baltic, through the endless forests and lakes on its northern and eastern shores, the teachings of Luther travelled swiftly to the more receptive centres. In the eastern trading cities, Riga, Reval and Dorpat, they found champions not only in the German merchants but also in the Teutonic Knights and the city councils, both already locked in jurisdictional conflicts with the Catholic bishops. As early as 1522 the knights and burghers made protests against the Edict of Worms and the excommunication of Luther. At Riga the chief emissary of the Evangelical cause was Andreas Knopken, the former pupil of Bugenhagen and a fellow-Pomeranian, who in June 1522 staged a disputation with his Catholic opponents. His performance induced the city council to renounce allegiance to the Archbishop and carry out a Reformation along Lutheran lines. In all three cities the problem of the Reformers was not to evoke but to restrain a radical spirit. In 1524–5 the mobs everywhere smashed images and even destroyed churches: at Reval this popular iconoclasm received added stimulus from a local feud between the city guilds and the Dominicans. In due course the three cities settled down under Lutheran church ordinances, the code drawn up at Reval in 1525 being among the earliest throughout the Lutheran world. Nevertheless, in the years that followed, these changes failed to produce larger political groupings or even to maintain the independence of the east Baltic communities: erelong Esthonia with Reval fell to Sweden, while Livonia with Riga and Dorpat became incorporated into Poland-Lithuania.

Few if any sixteenth-century politicians can have foreseen the far-reaching consequences of the extension of Lutheranism into Scandinavia, but it was to prove a crucial factor in the future history of the Baltic lands, of the German Protestant states, even of the Empire itself. When in 1628–9 Habsburg power under Wallenstein reached the shores of the Baltic, it became evident that the Reformation had found in Sweden a base which Wallenstein could not seize as he had just seized Jutland. More important still, it soon transpired that Protestantism had helped to forge a great power, able under the leadership of Gustavus Adolphus to roll back the southern Catholic armies from the whole of north Germany. The Diet of Västerås can hence be regarded as an early step on the long road toward the Treaty of Westphalia.

The German and Baltic areas we have now enumerated represent almost the whole of the permanent and outright conquests of the Evangelical religion. In many other regions of Europe it attracted numerous individuals, created congregations, yet failed to strike deep roots in society or to elicit from rulers and governing classes the co-operation so essential for the establishment of territorial churches. Yet in many cases the Lutheran Church found itself displaced not by Catholic reaction but by Calvinism, or by other systems owing debts to Luther's career. The full impact of that career upon Europe cannot be conveyed by a map of the areas finally subject to Lutheran church-government. For the intellectual and even the bourgeois classes of Europe outside Germany, Luther's doctrine needed to be presented afresh in clearer and more systematic form. This is substantially what Calvin had accomplished when in February 1535 he arranged for the publication of his *Religionis Christianae Institutio*. The subsequent story of his attempt to set up a 'perfect school of Christ' at Geneva is apt to distract our attention from the fact that his doctrine is so largely based on that of the Saxon Reformer, whom he regarded with an open and unswerving admiration.

In matters of religion as distinct from ecclesiastical politics, Calvin should be seen as Luther's continuator rather than as his supplanter. He spoke of Luther as "one whom I venerate with all my heart. We all, I confess, owe much to him." In 1545 Luther perused Calvin's tract *The Supper of the Lord*, and said to his Wittenberg bookseller, "He is certainly a learned and pious man. . . . If Oecolampadius and Zwingli had expressed themselves in this way at the beginning, we should never have been involved in so long a controversy." But it was as well for both that they admired one another at a distance! Despite differences of idiom, emphasis and method, Calvin did not regard himself as a rival but rather as the leader chosen to make Luther's message work in a shifting world, a world already very different from that of the year 1520, a world in which the message seemed endangered not merely by Catholic powers but by the spiritual indiscipline and muddled thinking of Protestantism itself. Calvin did not act either as if the Word were irresistible or as if civil states were hopelessly tainted. From the outset he believed not merely in evangelism but in the active association of ministers and magistrates to enforce Christian living. Rulers governed righteously when permeated by true religion, while there was nothing to debar ministers from exercising a real if indirect control over secular policy. Given this sort of influence, Calvin could believe, as Luther could not, in a 'Christian State'. Yet allowing for the fact that he worked mainly in the Switzerland of the forties and fifties, even the social and political doctrines of Calvin do not differ so profoundly from those of Luther. Calvin also taught non-resistance to tyranny, and while he allowed some loopholes he did not foresee or plan the subsequent revolts led by his adherents in France, the Netherlands and Scotland. In the event, his followers were called upon to bear the brunt of Catholic attack, and they were forced to become activists to avoid extinction. Their outlook on the world was changed above all by the harsh facts of political and military geography.

So far as the relations of God and man are concerned, Calvin's theological system is little more than a brilliant systematization of Luther's. It is strictly theocentric and Christocentric; likewise it rejects all forms of mysticism in favour of an austere emphasis on the biblical documents. It stresses with Luther the utter sovereignty of God, the divine predestination of all material and spiritual processes, the absence of any redemptive free-will in man, the powerlessness of the fallen creature to contribute a jot to his own salvation, his dependence upon the justifying power of God-given faith alone.

Calvinism taught men to worship, work and fight in the small community, but it was not a truly congregationalist or a sectarian religion. Calvin believed that God in his sovereignty could save a soul outside the Church, yet no one stressed more decisively than he the need for a strong Church, the context within which God in fact usually does save men.

To this picture of continuity between Luther and Calvin one major exception remains. In a world of unbalanced theological interests, the divergence of Calvin's eucharistic doctrine from that of Luther naturally bulked large. Calvin rejected Roman transubstantiation, Zwinglian symbolism and the so-called consubstantiation of Luther, yet in the last resort his own attempt to interpret Christ's intention at the Last Supper was eirenical rather than controversial. He was deeply influenced by the mediating position adopted by Martin Bucer. Despite his Zürich Agreement of 1549 with Zwingli's successor Bullinger, here he stood little nearer to Zwingli than to Luther. While refuting the Lutheran notion of the ubiquity of Christ's body, and while denying any change in the elements of bread and wine, he accorded a most positive and objective meaning to the promise that the faithful communicant should receive the power and virtue of Christ's body and blood. For him the spiritual reality is not enclosed within the elements, yet it is given at the same moment as they are given: the elements and the Spirit remain quite distinct, yet the physical action and the spiritual action take place together, as it were in parallel. While this doctrine provided the sacrament with a depth of meaning unrealised by Zwingli, it was also simpler to understand than Luther's doctrine of the eucharist. The latter remained indeed the shibboleth by which Lutheran orthodoxy recognised itself, yet this whole insoluble dispute gradually receded from the focus of popular Protestant interest as the century advanced.

However justifiable it may be to regard Calvin as the preserver and disseminator of Luther's basic message, it must nevertheless frankly be recognised that Calvin founded a separate series of churches, that these latter increasingly assumed the leadership of militant Protestantism, that the Lutheran Evangelical and the Calvinist Reformed often behaved as bitter rivals rather than as allies. On the other hand it is possible to exaggerate the practical effects of this rivalry. The expansion of Luther's direct influence was checked not merely by Calvinism but by a multitude of other inhibiting factors, many of them regional in character. Their strength is revealed even by the briefest examination of the conditions which the Reformation encountered in the various countries of Europe.

In so many respects France remained the greatest of the

nations, though her sixteenth-century rulers failed to mobilise her vast latent powers. In merely secular terms, a Reformation similar to that organised by Henry VIII in England would have given the restive gentry a share in the vast lands of the French Church, might perhaps have avoided the appalling civil wars which filled the second half of the century. During the twenties and early thirties public opinion showed signs of providing a basis for such a national Reformation. The spirit of humanist criticism and the Augustinian theology stimulated by Lefèvre opened the minds of many Frenchmen not merely to the need for reforms but to more specifically Protestant ideas. In February 1519 Froben reported that he had sent 600 copies of Luther's work into France, and from Paris in November 1520 the Swiss humanist Henri Loriti wrote to Zwingli:

> There are no books bought with greater avidity than those of Luther . . . One bookshop has sold 1400 . . . Everywhere people speak well of Luther, and yet the chain of the monks is a long one!

The condemnation of Luther's errors by the Sorbonne followed in April 1521; though it was backed by the Parlement, it ostensibly served only to increase the circulation of heretical books, some imported, others published covertly in France by Simon Dubois of Alençon and other Protestant printers. And while Lefèvre himself neither denounced the Papacy nor embraced the full gamut of Lutheran doctrine, among his admirers stood sterner men like Guillaume Farel, who was one day to call Calvin to reform Geneva; again, like Jacques Pavanes and Louis de Berquin, who not only turned Lutheran but went to the stake (1526, 1529) for their beliefs. They had been long preceded by the Norman Augustinian Jean Vallière, burned at Paris as early as August 1523. From 1520 groups denounced as Lutheran existed at Lyons and at Avignon, from which latter the Franciscan François Lambert fled (via Wittenberg and Strassburg) to become a prominent Reformer in Hesse. Meanwhile the famous German jurist Melchior Wolmar introduced Lutheranism to receptive audiences in the university of Bourges, then being attended by the young Calvin. By the mid-twenties a large number of provincial towns throughout most regions of France boasted active Protestant organisations. Modern scholars have also traced the specific influences of Luther upon many French writers of the period, even upon the anticlerical yet distinctly non-Lutheran Rabelais.

Nevertheless, until reinforced from Calvin's Geneva during the fifties, the Reformation in France was a diffuse and ill-led movement. It drew inspiration from a multitude of sources besides Luther; many Frenchmen notorious as *Luthériens* were really followers of Erasmus and Lefèvre, or else derived their ideas from Bucer, Zwingli, even from the Anabaptists or the Waldensians. Frenchmen did not resort to the University of Wittenberg, and Luther had no opportunity to build up a French missionary group. Until Calvin impinged upon the French scene, there appeared no great leader able to weld together all these movements or even to translate Protestant teachings into forms fully attractive to the French mind. In any case French society was not dominated by intellectuals; it was conservative and overwhelmingly rural, a society of bucolic peasants, *curés* and squires. As elsewhere, the towns produced the first Protestant groups, yet they lacked the social influence and the independent spirit which marked the great cities of the Holy Roman Empire. Unlike the Scandinavian and Baltic towns, those of France did not contain dominant groups of German merchants, Moreover, the active opposition proved unexpectedly formidable.

Even though subordinated to the monarchy, the French Church remained capable of defending itself in local actions; the bishops and a number of provincial councils at once persecuted heretics and tried to allay criticism by piecemeal reforms. In the Sorbonne a resolute group of Catholic theologians succeeded not only in ousting Protestant and Erasmian scholars but in making the university a leading centre of orthodox propaganda. Yet in the last resort the situation depended upon the use of its immense powers by the monarchy, and it was to Francis I that Calvin hopefully addressed his *Institutio*. Francis had after all intrigued persistently with the German Lutheran princes, while his sister Marguérite had actually patronised not only Lefèvre but a fairly wide assortment of enthusiasts and eccentrics. By 1535, however, the worldly king resolved upon hostile action, in part provoked by the insult offered him the previous year at Amboise, when a rude Protestant affixed a placard to his bedroom door. The royal persecution which followed was intermittent, yet it helped to break up the chief nuclei of heresy and to postpone large-scale conversions until twenty years later, when Calvin was to unleash the full force of his numerous French graduates upon their native country.

Meanwhile in Spain and in Italy the situation remained less promising still. Even in Spain, it is true, the monarchical reform of the Church made under the guidance of Ximenes had not eradicated anticlericalism. Yet these reforms were matched by a genuine Catholic fervour which owed much to the stimulus of the long crusade against the Moors. In a country where even St. Ignatius and St. Theresa fell foul of the Inquisition, it remains difficult to distinguish the real Lutherans amid the crowd of Erasmians, Scripture-readers, anticlericals, liberals and mystics who were labelled Lutheran by this egregious organisation. Certainly there were individual Spaniards attracted by the Saxon heresy: men like Domingo de Rojas, who circulated Wittenberg books, like Augustin Cazalla and Francisco de San Roman, who had both encountered Lutheranism while travelling in Germany, like Francisco de Enzinas (Dryander), who along with a number of Spaniards took refuge in the Protestant England of Edward VI. That in mid-sixteenth century Spain there were groups influenced by Luther cannot be denied, yet it would be misleading to speak of a Spanish Lutheran movement. On the eve of Luther's advent, the Inquisition seemed about to undergo papal reforms at the demand of the indignant Cortes. Then the widespread fear of the new heresy gave it a new lease of life. Favoured by the withdrawal from Spain of the humanist court in 1529, it had things much its own way and drove into exile even innocent Catholic liberals like Pedro de Lerma, first Chancellor of Alcalá, the university founded by Ximenes himself. When in 1556–8 the Emperor Charles spent his retirement in Spain, he had become an advocate of harsh repression. And by 1570 his son Philip had almost extirpated those heresies which had debts to Lutheranism.

In the very different atmosphere of Italy, Lutheran books were indeed widely read by intellectuals, while anticlerical Venice refused to persecute the many visiting and resident Lutherans who contributed to her wealth. Nevertheless the tightening military grip of Spain discouraged religious experimentation among the ruling classes of the Italian states, while the new reforming spirit in the religious orders weakened without wholly destroying the inclination of disgruntled monks and friars to think in revolutionary terms. As for the old Waldensian heresy, it lacked the modern ideas and techniques—especially that of printing—which might have enabled it to break out in mass from its Alpine valleys or to multiply its secret congregations elsewhere in Italy. It could do little more than ally itself to Zwinglian and Calvinist missionaries when in due course they arrived.

Speaking generally, the spirit of Renaissance Italy lay poles apart from that of Luther. The educated classes were intellectual and curious rather than fervent or indignant; their capacities for a personal religion could as easily be occupied by Platonist speculation as by a quest for Christian assurance. Italian grievances and aspirations did not coincide with those of Luther's Germany. The hatreds provoked by the Papacy were only in rare cases founded upon religious zeal; even insofar as they were political, they lacked the deep resentments felt and expressed by German nationalism. While Italy provided the Reformation with a number of distinguished recruits like Pietro Martire Vermigli and Bernardino Ochino, its more characteristic response to the stresses of the age may be seen in that aristocratic and precious circle of choice spirits founded in Naples by Juan de Valdés. And when practical criticisms arose from eminent and virtuous men like Contarini, the offer of a cardinalate appeared no mere bribe but a brilliant opportunity to join in the work of Catholic reform.

Within the teutonic Netherlands, especially in the great cosmopolis of Antwerp with its numerous printing presses, its dominant mercantile class, its anticlericalism, its Germans,

Lutheran beliefs discovered a far more congenial home. Those beliefs not only laid the foundations of Netherlandish Protestantism but made Antwerp a major base for further advances. William Tyndale and other translators worked there under the patronage of the English merchant-colony to create the English Scriptures, and the city became the very cradle of English Protestantism. Yet in the Netherlands Luther's cause encountered a host of obstacles. The old-established radical and spiritualist wings of the Netherlandish *devotio moderna*, seemingly a 'natural' leadership, in fact found Luther's theology too conservative and too objectively scriptural for its tastes. Moreover, his sharply defined dogma seems to have proved unattractive to that large section of the Netherlandish public affected by the emotional tenor of the *devotio*.

More concrete threats arose from the active and unremitting opposition of the Emperor, who ruled by far the greater part of these provinces directly and by hereditary title. Here he did not need to display the restraint forced upon him by the German situation, and as early as July 1523 his government burned the two Augustinian friars Henry Voes and John Esch. These earliest martyrs of the Lutheran faith became the subject of Luther's hymn, *Ein neues Lied*. Nevertheless the Brussels authorities drove moderate Protestantism underground at a heavy cost, for at this time Anabaptism began pouring in, and greatly aided by unemployment in the northern shipping and weaving towns, it proved itself better adapted to assume the leadership of a desperate and proscribed Reformation. So the way opened first to the Dutch participation in the disaster at Münster, then later on, when Anabaptism was in its turn checked by persecution, to a new situation from which Calvinist missionaries and militants could best prosper. At the end of this chain came the Netherlands Revolt, a movement increasingly headed by the Calvinist minority and resulting at last in the withdrawal of the northern provinces from Habsburg rule.

In a situation like that of the Netherlands Lutheranism found difficulty in working underground, and in growing upwards from the roots of society. Even so, this also proved true of other great religious movements of the age. In many parts of Europe the Counter-Reformation itself would certainly have foundered without the vital help it received from Catholic rulers. Proscribed religions could spread widely, yet they could not stabilise their gains without enlisting the classes that actually controlled the machine of state or could somehow grasp its levers. In the Netherlands, in Scotland, in France, in Poland, Calvinism itself had to accomplish this feat in order to win any sort of ordered existence. A religion could not thrive purely upon popular appeal. Sixteenth-century societies were conservative, and the dominant classes frequently able to manipulate and canalise popular emotions. Even in those areas subject to civil and religious revolution, when the tumult and the shouting died, the old leadership (or something very like it) was still found sitting in the saddle and issuing the orders.

The relations of England with Lutheranism (as with so many continental movements) had a wholly unique character. During the earlier twenties the Augustinian friar Robert Barnes headed at Cambridge the first English group which can properly be called Protestant. He was a genuine Lutheran, who after his escape from English persecutors spent some time in Wittenberg. There he was especially helped by the ever-enterprising Bugenhagen, who was in touch with other early English disciples. In his published works Barnes constantly reproduced Luther. During the thirties under the semi-Protestant control of Thomas Cromwell and Archbishop Cranmer, he moderated his more radical expressions and served the government as an envoy to the Lutheran states. When at last he fell along with Cromwell and was burned for heresy in the Catholic reaction of 1539–40, Luther himself tenderly referred to him as 'St. Robert'. Likewise William Tyndale, a significant pamphleteer as well as a great translator, visited Wittenberg and was never more in his element than when translating Luther. Through Tyndale's fine version of Luther's famous *Prologue to Romans*, many English readers first met in succinct and striking form the fully-fledged theology of the Saxon Reformer. Nevertheless, some even of this first generation of English Protestants soon began to diverge from the Lutheran norms. In 1530 Tyndale turned from the New Testament to the translation of the Pentateuch, and thenceforth his own theology developed a stronger emphasis upon Law, as opposed to Luther's emphasis upon Gospel. A sinner was still indeed justified before God by faith, yet he was thenceforth justified before man through obedience to the Law of God. By 1534 Tyndale was sketching in very bald terms a covenant-theology whereby God's fulfilment of his promises became contingent upon man's fulfilment of the Law.

This modified system had its Continental analogies in the writings of Oecolampadius, Bucer, Bullinger and others: along with other features of the English religious scene it fore-shadowed the moralist approaches of the Puritans. The most ori-ginal English theologian of these years, the young martyr John Frith, did not in fact modify Luther's theocentric and solifidian positions, but his best work concerned the eucharist, and here he adopted radical positions derived in part from Oecolampa-dius and Zwingli. Such non-Lutheran tendencies increased rather than diminished as the English Reformation developed. Thomas Cranmer, travelling in 1532 on an embassy to the Emperor, married a niece of the eminent Lutheran divine Andreas Osiander. Yet despite his close relations with the Lutheran world, Cranmer's liturgical experiments culminating in the Prayer Books of 1549 and 1552 drew upon a wide range of ideas, both Catholic and Protestant. He was much more in-fluenced by Bucer than by Luther, but in addition he and his theological adviser Nicholas Ridley thought for themselves and were well versed in the earlier sources, biblical, patristic and medieval.

Luther had behaved most rudely toward Henry VIII, and when the latter's divorce induced him at last to break with Rome, he developed little personal interest in the possibility of a Protestant Reformation. Even so, the Augsburg Confession and the Wittenberg Articles of 1536 exercised some influence upon the various formularies of faith set forth by Henry and his successors, culminating in the Thirty-Nine Articles of Elizabeth. Again, Henry's near-Lutheran advisers Cromwell and Cranmer induced him in 1537 to allow the circulation of Bibles trans-lated by Protestants, and two years later to set forth an official English Bible, in reality the work of Tyndale and Tyndale's former collaborator Miles Coverdale. At Cromwell's instigation Henry permitted desultory negotiations with the Elector of Saxony and the Schmalkaldic League, but he would neither allow the Germans to instruct him in theology nor become the paymaster of a European Protestant alliance. Cromwell's final attempt to tie him to Lutheran allies through the Cleves marriage cost the unfortunate minister his head and opened the way to the partial reaction of Henry's last years. The doctrinal and liturgical eclecticism of the English divines, the pragmatic and erastian outlook of the Tudor public, Henry's pride in his own theological learning and his persistent refusal to imitate foreign models, these and other factors had now set England upon a course that steadily diverged from that of the Lutheran world.

From the reign of Edward VI, when Bucer, Pietro Martire, Ochino and so many other non-Lutheran refugees flocked to England, the fresh inspirations of English Protestantism came not from Wittenberg but from Strassburg, Zürich and Geneva. Then during the Catholic reaction of Queen Mary most of the 800 English Protestant refugees found welcoming hands not in the places owing spiritual allegiance to Wittenberg but in Switzerland, Strassburg and Frankfurt. These exiles were influential people and in 1558–9 they returned home to dominate the Anglican Settlement. There are signs that at this stage the young Queen Elizabeth would have preferred, both doctrinally and politically, a solution nearer to that of the Lutheran monarchies, but the desirability of rapid agreement impelled her to compromise with the returned exiles, whose notions of Protestantism had not ripened in Lutheran backgrounds.

Through the English more than through any other people the Reformation was destined in future centuries to achieve extra-European influence. English Calvinist Puritanism, the English sects, Anglicanism and Methodism alike took full advantage of the immense colonial and mercantile expansion of the subsequent centuries. The failure of Lutheranism to capture England during the mid-Tudor period hence became a negative fact of much significance in world history. Through this failure its development outside Europe began later in the day and proceeded along less massive, less historically influential lines than did that of English Protestantism.

While continental Saxony provided a poor base for an attack upon the Atlantic world, it was far better situated in regard to eastern Europe. There the three kingdoms of Poland, Bohemia and Hungary seemed in many respects well prepared to hear Luther's appeal. Despite the weakness of their elective monarchies and the great power of their territorial nobles, they were far from being barbaric frontier-states remote from the new influences besetting the mind of Europe. Both in their court life and among their educated clerics and aristocrats, Italianate humanist scholarship and classical influences in art and architecture had established themselves. Far more books were being printed in Poland than, for example, in England. While the universities of Prague and Cracow themselves enjoyed international reputations, every year thousands of young eastern nobles left home to attend the universities of Germany and the western countries. Many came from huge estates made wealthy by the growing function of the east as the granary of Europe. They had the means and the backgrounds conducive to mental emancipation. Amongst these modish aristocrats, anticlericalism extended far beyond the moralist ridicule which they found in the writings of Erasmus and the German humanists. Nowhere more than in Poland did the lay ruling classes resent the tax-exemptions claimed by the clergy and the severe punishments meted out by the universally-hated ecclesiastical courts.

On the other hand the three kingdoms all contained elements neutral or inhospitable toward Lutheranism. While strong German groups existed in several Polish towns, neither they nor their native fellow townsmen could exert wide political or social influence. In Transylvania the rapid acceptance of Luther's doctrines by the large but unpopular communities of German settlers did not endear those doctrines to the Magyar inhabitants. Among Slavs and Magyars in general, Germans were apt to appear as colonisers, and the strongly teutonic flavour of Lutheranism tended to arouse sentimental linguistic and cultural opposition. Moreover, the Polish and Hungarian gentry were Latin-educated; far more readily than Luther's German works they assimilated those of Zwingli and Calvin, which came to them in this more familiar dress. Again, Calvinism offered land-owning magnates a much more active and desirable rôle than that suggested by the Lutheran church ordinances. Like the great Huguenot peers of France, the Polish nobles could control, or themselves become, the lay elders of the Calvinist congregations. Yet while the Reformed principles of Geneva overtook Lutheranism and made a deeper impression upon Poland, there the general tenor of thought remained strikingly tolerant. Religion varied from estate to estate, from province to province. Soon after the mid-century a fully-fledged Presbyterian order existed in Little Poland and in Lithuania, while in Great Poland the Lutherans held a much stronger position. Liberal Catholic monarchs like Sigismund Augustus (1548–72) and Stephen Báthory (Prince of Transylvania, 1571; King of Poland, 1575–86) maintained friendly relations with both Protestant camps. By their time the Jesuits were beginning the great reconquest of Poland, while at the other extreme a number of magnates were fostering Unitarianism, a new child of Renaissance rationalism which had its most notorious European centre at Rakow. Thus in Poland there developed a situation which Martin Luther at his most imaginative could never have foretold.

In Bohemia the early Lutheran emissaries beheld a very different scene. The old divisions among the Hussites remained as deep as ever, but from the first Luther welcomed both the conservative groups and the Bohemian Brethren as brother Evangelicals. With the latter he came to an agreement on the eucharist by the year 1542. On the other hand the Hussite puritans known as Amosites linked naturally with the Anabaptists, who from the early twenties came out of the German-speaking lands to Bohemia, and in still greater numbers to Moravia. Luther's relations with the Hussite world should be regarded as a *rapprochement* rather than a conquest; the country never became thoroughly Lutheranised, while even among the conservative Hussites many refused to surrender their ecclesiastical identity, feeling that their older traditions obviated any need for substantial changes in Luther's direction. Again, as the tragic events of the Thirty Years War were to demonstrate, such religious links as were established did not lead to solid political links; they failed to ensure that in time of crisis the Lutheran princes and the Bohemian nobles would pursue a common policy toward their common foes the Habsburgs. So often in central European history Habsburg dynasticism prevailed against what seem to us the more obvious dictates of common sense and self-interest.

In Hungary the first impact of Lutheranism was swiftly followed (1526) by the disaster of Mohács. The kingdom soon fell into three parts: a western strip under King Ferdinand, a central area occupied by the Turks, and to the east Transylvania under John Zápolyai. This situation, desperate enough for the nation itself, contained some features favourable to the inroads of Protestantism. Neither Ferdinand nor Zápolyai could afford to persecute those nobles and towns which accepted the latter. As for the Turks, they despised all forms of Christianity and in their contempt allowed free movement to all sorts of missionaries. Most of the Catholic bishops had actually been slain on the field of Mohács; everywhere the surviving priesthood suffered miserable poverty and remained discredited and ineffective until the coming of the Counter-Reformation. Nevertheless, for the reasons we have adumbrated, Lutheranism did not make very rapid progress except among the 'Saxons' of Transylvania. In the slightly longer run the Calvinist missionaries salvaged far more from the rubble of national disaster, a fact attested to this day by their preponderant situation amongst the Protestant communities of Hungary. In 1561 the so-called *Confessio Catholica* established strict Calvinist doctrine throughout those many areas where the nobles, their peasants, and even some townsmen (as at Debrecen) looked for inspiration to Geneva. In Translyvania the election of Stephen Báthory preserved Catholicism, but here as in Poland all the faiths—Catholicism, Lutheranism, Calvinism, Unitarianism— had to be recognised by public authority. And if a man did not like the local worship he could often escape to another area where the local magnates shared his religious convictions. But here as throughout the three countries the Lutheran churches failed to establish an ascendancy proof against the new forces which gradually revealed themselves through the middle and later decades of the century. In Scandinavia strong monarchs, little hampered by anti-German traditions and operating in relative peace and geographical isolation, had tipped the balance in favour of the Lutheran solution. None of these decisive features can be detected in the tragic history of the nations on Europe's great eastern plains.

Chapter Seven

Luther's last years and the Augsburg Settlement, c.1540–1555

DURING Luther's last years his movement had not yet ceased to expand, but its growth-rate had diminished. Outside Germany and German communities it had found many novel, even inhospitable situations; it had tended to become over-dependent upon the vagaries of secular support. Untoward circumstances and unimaginative local leadership may indeed be blamed for some of its checks and defeats, yet by this time even its most eminent figures had become involved in errors of judgment and statesmanship. The affair concerning Philip of Hesse touched the credit and honour of Luther himself. Whatever his limitations, this bold prince had rendered sterling services to Protestantism, and even the story of his marital affairs commands some little degree of sympathy. At the age of nineteen he had been married to Christina, daughter of Duke George of Saxony. Repelled, as he claimed, by her disgusting habits, he kept mistresses and contracted venereal disease, from which he was partly cured in 1539 by Martin Bucer's friend Gereon Sailer of Augsburg. His already troubled conscience had now been further exacerbated by suffering. By belief a staunch Evangelical, he feared damnation for the vice which he could not shake off, and he refrained from taking communion lest it should increase his guilt. But this spiritual modesty did not prevent him from reading the Bible and discovering that certain Old Testament patriarchs had practised bigamy (and even polygamy) without attracting the divine wrath. He also made the mistake of falling in love with one of his sister's ladies, Margaret von der Saal, who refused to live with him except in open and lawful matrimony. Her ambitious mother even demanded that Luther, Bucer and Melanchthon, or at least two of them, together with envoys of the Elector and the Duke of Saxony, should be present as witnesses at the marriage.

At this conjuncture Gereon Sailer went to Strassburg and gradually involved the impressionable Martin Bucer in Philip's problems. Unaware that the Landgrave was actually planning a bigamous marriage, Bucer journeyed to Wittenberg to enlist the support of Luther and Melanchthon, who likewise received only an expurgated account of the facts. They interpreted St. Matthew to the effect that Christ had permitted divorce only on the ground of adultery, but they were sorry for Philip and anxious to help him in what appeared a genuine problem of conscience. And it was easy to think of themselves as granting a dispensation in a very exceptional case, comparable with those of princes whose problems had been from time to time sympathetically adjudged by Rome. The document extracted from them by Bucer and known as the Wittenberg *Rathschlag* is hardly a dispensation to commit bigamy: it is mainly devoted to dissuading the Landgrave from that course. It nevertheless admits that the practice existed among the Old Testament patriarchs, and that it is not in so many words forbidden by the Gospels. And it weakly concludes that if Philip is unalterably determined to take another wife, he must assume responsibility, and to avoid scandal keep the affair secret. When ultimately the wedding with Margaret von der Saal occurred, Melanchthon graced it with his presence.

In the opinion of some high-minded scholars, the Wittenbergers committed no misdemeanours as theologians. On the other hand, that they displayed political folly could hardly be denied by their warmest admirers. Despite these devious precautions the secret was soon noised abroad: Philip found himself confronted by the very severe Imperial law directed against bigamy and he called upon Luther to defend him in public. This the Reformer declined to do, on the ground that advice given a man in the secrecy of the confessional did not involve a disclaimer of public law; the consequences of this law the man must face on his own responsibility. As on other occasions, Luther's brutally frank expressions gave his foes ample opportunity to exaggerate his part in the affair, but when the full facts were disclosed, the personal stigma attaching to the divines was by no means the main casualty for Protestantism. Threatened with the possibility of deposition, Philip of Hesse resolved to seek the friendship of the Emperor. The latter (who had been careful to exclude his own promiscuous adulteries from public life) naturally demanded a high price for his favour: that Philip should no longer support his Protestant allies in future negotiations about the faith, and that he should hinder those allies from forming leagues with foreign powers. To these conditions the Landgrave finally agreed at the Diet of Regensburg in 1541, and the first major wedge was driven into the Protestant structure. Others were soon to follow.

Intelligibly enough, these blunders have been held to typify the lack of poise and calculation which marked the behaviour of the ageing and ailing Luther. From his fortieth year his illnesses had been frequent, varied and sometimes severe. Intermittently he suffered from sleeplessness, digestive troubles, catarrh, severe pains in the head, haemorrhoids, nervous contractions of the chest, and at least one chronic attack of the stone. He rested or obeyed doctors' orders only insofar as immediate necessity demanded, for he set no store whatever on prolonging his life. From about the time of his marriage he rapidly put on weight; the paunchy and heavy-jowled figure of the later years bears little resemblance to that of the gaunt young monk. Even by 1530 he presented what one clinical observer has called 'a perfect case of neurasthenia or premature old age'.

The life of a writer takes a far greater physical toll than is generally realised, and Luther's problems sprang in no small part from an effort hardly paralleled in the annals of literature. In less than thirty years he produced over 350 printed works, quite apart from his innumerable letters and unprinted memoranda. Even in years when he lost time through illness and travel his output remained almost unbelievable. His illnesses brought no impairment of his mental faculties, and he shows no genuinely psychopathic tendencies, whatever the allegations of certain modern critics. That he ascribed his depressions and ailments to visitations of the Devil was in that age no sign of neurosis, let alone insanity: both St. Ignatius and St. Theresa had to contend with far more vivid demonic apparitions, but no one has called them psychopaths. Again, every piece of alleged evidence for drunkenness, gluttony and vice conjured up by Denifle was long ago (1904–18) disproved by Boehmer in the expanding editions of his scholarly work *Luther in the Light of Modern Research*. The Reformer admittedly injured a naturally sound constitution by living too hard, yet it was in more honourable ways than these. Despite his geniality and kindliness, his underlying disposition was choleric; he felt anger more than is good for mind or body, and unlike most rebels, he did not feel it less acutely with advancing middle age. This emotion he worked off not by immoderate or cruel conduct but by violent writing. His aggressive, sometimes obscene outbursts should not, however, be linked too closely with his physical and nervous decline. It must first be seen in relation to the extreme coarseness of the period, of which countless literary examples may be placed alongside those furnished by Luther. In addition, one must recall that violence appears often enough in Luther's earlier writings, while on the other hand he could sometimes write with serenity and moderation to the end of his life.

In all conscience, the violence remains obtrusive enough in the ceaseless pamphleteering of the later years. The scholars of Louvain and Paris are 'filthy swine, lecherous Epicurean pigs, cesspits bubbling with hell-fire'. He renews his savage assaults on the Catholic princes, Duke George, Albert of Mainz, and especially on 'Jack Sausage', the Catholic Duke Henry of Brunswick, who in 1541 attracted Luther's wrath by an attack on the Landgrave Philip. In 1543 the Reformer matched these vitriolic performances with a literary assault upon the Jews, though twenty years earlier he had protested in the strongest terms against persecution as the greatest obstacle to winning them for Christianity. The pamphlet *Of the Jews and their Lies* must of course be seen in a sixteenth-century context: for example, alongside the cruel persecution of the Jews in Spain and the creation of a ghetto in Rome in 1557. Anti-Semitism was one of the many un-Christian aspects of medieval Christian society, and here the elderly Luther merely failed to transcend his mental environment. He did not originate new emotional vices, while his dislike of the Jews had little in common with the secular racialism of recent times. His greatest violence he continued to reserve for the old enemy. The pamphlet *Against the Papacy at Rome, founded by the Devil* (1545) made Bullinger say that he had never read anything more 'savage or imprudent'. It was embellished by a series of caricatures by Cranach on 'the Ass and Swine of a Pope', and by some verses of Luther's own which it would be charitable to describe as coarse. His lack of realism went beyond his naïve supposition that the Papacy was doomed beyond all hope of recovery. He still liked to think he was defending both Emperor and Empire against the renewed assaults of the Antichrist in Rome.

Of all his associates Luther most loved and admired his natural complement, Philip Melanchthon. "I must root out the trunks and stems . . . I am the rough woodman who has to make a path, but Philip goes quietly and peacefully along it, builds and plants, sows and waters at his pleasure." Nevertheless the divergence of approach had long since revealed itself as something rather more than a matter of methods and personalities. Melanchthon's humanist upbringing had penetrated beyond any mere style and technique. While fully accepting salvation by the imputed merits of Christ, and clearly distinguishing between this process and the process of man's renewal or sanctification, he found it hard to follow the stark radicalism with which in 1525 Luther had denied to mankind every sort of saving initiative and merit. The disciple who had found such exquisite phrases to express Luther's great doctrines now laid increasing stress upon the Catholic concept of salvation as a transformation of character. A humanist who had never lost contact with Luther's antagonist Erasmus, Philip sought to tame and civilise mankind. "I have never been a theologian," he said, "except in order to reform life." In the deepest sense, he still admitted God to be omnipotent, man helpless apart from God-given faith. Yet must not man be allowed to possess a 'natural light' whereby he can discern the truths exposed to his gaze? And in view of the universal decline of conduct, should not Evangelical Christians be sensitive to the charge of antinomianism, of moral fatalism, so often levelled against them? Had not God begun to lay the foundations of man's salvation in the teaching of heathen philosophers long before the coming of Christ? And whereas Luther's spiritual agonies had left their victim humbly accepting the mysterious contradictions of the divine scheme, Philip had passed through no such agonies. His tidy, tabulating, academic mind craved a coherent structure; he judged a doctrine by its place in the intellectual scheme rather than by its services to the life of religion or by its healing power in his own experience. Having at first followed Luther in rejecting the scholastic models, he then laid the foundations of a remarkable era of Protestant scholasticism and made Reason once more a source of theology co-ordinate with Revelation. No sooner had Luther hurled the heathen Aristotle from the porch than Melanchthon readmitted him by the back door. Meanwhile the *Loci Communes*, at first based solely on the Bible, incorporated with each successive edition more of the Fathers and the Schoolmen.

Like Zwingli, Philip longed to believe in the salvation of the virtuous heathen; like Aquinas, he wanted to reconcile natural philosophy and Christian dogma; like so many other 'enlightened' Christian leaders, he tried to discover how far the rigours of Pauline theology could be adjusted to the advancing thought of a 'contemporary' world. This last adjustment involved him with the Graeco-Roman revival, with the natural sciences, with modern political necessities, with rival Protestant movements, even with a Catholic orthodoxy which condescended to debate with him and even began showing signs of self-reform. Melanchthon's theological departure revealed itself when in the 1535 edition of his *Loci Communes* he denied the total impotence of the human will and, by the doctrine later known as Synergism, assigned to that will a certain rôle in the process of conversion. His view of the eucharist also began to show flexibility. Having at first upheld Luther's doctrine, he seemed in the 1540 version of the Augsburg Confession (*Confessio Augustana Variata*) to be moving toward a more symbolic and spiritual doctrine similar to those of Bucer and Calvin. This shift later on enabled the Lutheran rigorists, who never understood Melanchthon's type of idealism, to call his followers not merely Philipists but Crypto-Calvinists.

Philip's theological liberalism did not extend far into his political and social theory. Appalled by the supposed collapse of morality, in particular by the 'wild and untamed' character of the German people, he glorified the secular State, including the institution of serfdom, in terms which Luther would not have used. While his State was based on the overriding rule of law, and while he preferred city oligarchs to princes, he failed to set up safeguards against princely tyranny. For good or ill Melanchthon's influence upon German intellectual, social and political life was to prove very great throughout the centuries to come. At the very outset, at the very heart of the movement, this very able mind was at work to subdue the teaching of Luther and subtly moderate its heavy element of protest. During the last years of Luther's life relations between the two tended at times to become strained. Yet Melanchthon never pressed matters to extremes. He reverenced Luther and feared his anger; in their relationship there appears to the end a strong suggestion of master and gifted pupil. As for Luther, his genius for friendship could be just as deep and just as irrational as his genius for hatred. By a strange and rather charming irony, while Luther lived Melanchthon could be sure of protection against the gathering storm of Lutheran orthodoxy.

Quite apart from the sectarians and spiritualists, certain of Luther's own followers clashed with his views during his lifetime. One of these was Johann Agricola, his fellow-native of Eisleben and his former secretary during the Leipzig debates. Orthodox Lutheranism had always made much of the antithesis between Gospel and Law, meaning by the latter both the moral law implanted in the conscience, and the Mosaic Law superseded by Christ. Luther nevertheless held that the Law still had a part to play, as initially convincing men of their sin and begetting repentance. In 1537 Agricola aroused him by maintaining that the Gospel alone covered the whole process of conversion and salvation, that this whole concept of the Law was unevangelical and reactionary. He even coined the slogan:

"To the gallows with Moses." This seemed to the Wittenberg theologians closely akin to antinomianism, the charge often made against themselves by their Catholic foes. There followed three years of theses and counter-theses, interspersed with brief and superficial reconciliations. The faults lay on both sides. The unheroic Agricola knew that he and his family depended on Luther for subsistence; he made timid submissions, but then returned to the attack. Luther, at first tolerant, ended by developing a fierce resentment against this second-rater, this vain and incorrigible disciple who ventured so pertinaciously to dispute his authority. Here Luther proved far from amenable to the rights of conscience in others, and he was fully backed by the other leading Wittenbergers, who reported to the Elector in exaggerated terms on the perils of antinomianism. But even as that ruler in 1540 started proceedings against Agricola, the latter was rescued by an invitation from the Elector Joachim II of Brandenburg, who summoned him to serve as a court preacher in Berlin.

In his last years Luther was also troubled by deviationism on the part of a more distinguished old friend. This was Andreas Osiander of Nuremberg, who elaborated a theory of justification more akin to Augustine's than to Luther's. He maintained that justification meant no mere imputation of Christ's merits, but an *inhabitatio Christi* in the soul of the believer, involving a substantial transfer of actual righteousness. Yet another sort of criticism arose from the Wittenberg jurist Hieronymus Schurf, who had been one of the official Saxon advisers to Luther at the Diet of Worms. This man had been a sufferer from exaggerated scruples of conscience; more important, while he fully accepted Luther's theology, he now demanded episcopacy and the restoration of the canon law; he disputed the validity of the orders conferred on Lutheran pastors and even Luther's own right to marry! Faced by all these opinionated characters, Luther querulously asked Philip Melanchthon, "How many different masters will men be following in a hundred years' time?" He was addressing the right man!

These internal rifts among the Lutherans were but one aspect of Protestantism's general failure to attain the cohesion demanded by the coming crisis. The superficial Wittenberg Concord of 1536 between Luther and Bucer produced little active collaboration between their respective parties; it certainly did not prevent Luther from using hard words when Bucer's sacramental teachings prevailed at Cologne and elsewhere. The equally striking case for co-operation with the Swiss was hardly advanced by Luther, when in his *Short Confession of the Supper* (1544) he spoke of the Zwinglians as 'soul-destroyers and heretics'. But nemesis was first to take a political and military form, and in their own field the Lutheran princes were setting their theologians too few examples of restraint and wisdom. In particular, the acceptance of the Reformation by Ducal Saxony had failed to allay the grave rivalries between the Albertine house at Dresden and the Ernestines at Wittenberg. From this continuing rift even more than from the blunders of Philip of Hesse the future troubles of the Schmalkaldic League were to spring. Had the Lutherans possessed greater foresight, they might have taken alarm not merely from the obvious Habsburg menace, but from the signs of reform in the Roman Church, especially when after the accession of Paul III in 1534 the new spirit began to penetrate the pagan citadel of the Curia. By 1538 the Pope had nominated the critical prelates Contarini, Sadoleto, Caraffa, Pole and Aleander to the Sacred College.

Meanwhile the Papacy prepared a last effort to contain the Lutheran problem by direct diplomacy. In 1535 the nuncio Paul Vergerio (who in later life defected to Lutheranism) was sent to interview Luther and other Protestant leaders, and he was able to report their continued willingness to attend a conference. Supported by the Emperor, these initiatives led to the famous meetings held first at Hagenau and Worms, and then in April–May 1541 alongside the Diet at Regensburg. To these gatherings the Emperor invited among others Melanchthon, Bucer and Johann Pistorius of Hesse. On the other side of the table sat the two liberal Catholic theologians Johannes Gropper and Julius von Pflug; and though they were accompanied by the intransigent Eck, he was kept under control by the legate Contarini, himself as strong a champion of justification by faith as a papalist could then be, and one with a personal history of crisis and conversion not wholly remote from that of Luther. On this occasion Melanchthon took a firmer line than hitherto, and it has been conjectured that he was encouraged by the young John Calvin, who attended as a member of the Strassburg delegation. Surprisingly enough, the two sides did achieve a common formula upon justification, as well as upon a number of less controversial issues. Yet chasms remained which no mere good will could bridge. Seen in retrospect, Regensburg cannot be regarded even as a forlorn hope of reunion, if only because Contarini, widely suspected as half-Protestant, no more truly represented the Papacy than Melanchthon represented the increasingly dogmatic trend among the north German divines.

The way was now left open to the politicians and soldiers. Though in 1541 the Emperor stood in no position to follow words by blows, the obstacles gradually cleared from his path, and by the summer of 1543 he had already won an important success in north-west Germany. The young Duke William of Jülich-Cleves, whose sisters had married Henry VIII and John Frederick of Saxony, betrothed himself to a niece of the King of France and announced his acceptance of the Reformation. Moreover, he claimed to have inherited the duchy of Guelders, thereby gravely impeding the unification of the Netherlands under Habsburg rule. Faced by this array of threats, the Emperor swiftly isolated and defeated the Duke, causing him to cede the disputed territory and renounce his plan to enter the Protestant camp.

Despite this striking episode, Charles still confronted an Empire in which all the lay electors (now virtually joined by the Archbishop of Cologne) were known favourers of the Reformation. But by 1544 he managed to conclude the Peace of Crespy with France and to improve his relations with some of the princes, among them the half-Catholic Elector of Brandenburg. Meanwhile Duke William of Bavaria in the hope of promotion to an electorate agreed to a dynastic marriage between his son and the daughter of King Ferdinand. The most crucial stage arrived, however, when Charles made a wide breach in the Protestant front by forming an alliance with the ambitious young Duke Maurice of Albertine Saxony. While pursuing a decisive policy of Reformation in his own territories, Maurice had failed to heal the family rift with the Elector John Frederick. By joining the Emperor, he hoped to supplant his relative in the Saxon electorate and to receive in addition the ecclesiastical territories of Magdeburg and Halberstadt. Faced by these ugly developments, John Frederick and the other members of the Schmalkaldic League (rejoined by Philip of Hesse in 1544) were obliged to prepare for war, and though from the first Charles maintained that they should be punished for disobedience to the secular laws of the Empire, no one doubted that religion also had a share in the quarrel. Pope Paul openly treated the impending Habsburg attack as a crusade against heretics, and he contributed handsomely to the Emperor's funds.

On the gloomy eve of the conflict, as Germany watched and waited, the greatest yet most reluctant of its authors passed from the scene. Worn by public cares and by sickness, Luther had continued to drive himself remorselessly, often sitting at his desk for days and nights together. Without losing faith in his mission and in the future of his movement, he was expressing his weariness of the world and his readiness to leave it as soon as God should so decide. In the event his death was hastened by a mission to compose the bitter family quarrel raging in 1545 between the two Counts of Mansfeld. This little state was his home-country, and he felt a special duty to respond, even when called upon to make an arduous journey of some eighty miles in the depth of winter. Accompanied by his sons Martin and Paul, he left Wittenberg on 23 January, 1546, and was joined by Justus Jonas at Halle. Floods then held up the party, which did not arrive at Eisleben until the evening of 28 January. Utterly exhausted, Luther revived after a hot bath and massage, dined jovially with the quarrelsome family and was lodged in a house not far from his own birthplace. There followed three weeks of trying argument alongside the Counts and their legal advisers. As usual he preached several times and took part in communion and ordination services. On 17 February, the day when the dispute was at last settled in a friendly spirit, Luther was overtaken by a series of heart attacks and died during the night. During the intervals of his suffering he recited passages from the Scriptures, and when Jonas asked whether he was willing to die in the name of Christ and in the doctrine he had preached, he responded with a distinct affirmative, heard by all those present.

The final scenes befitted the immense importance of his career. At many points along the slow homeward journey great crowds of mourners gathered. Into Wittenberg there flocked a still greater concourse to follow Katherine Luther and her children to the funeral service at the Castle Church. The cortège entered by the same door on which thirty years earlier Luther had posted his Theses. Preaching the sermon, Bugenhagen eulogised him as a national hero of the German people. He had feared no one, however mighty. Though he might seem to have reproved and denounced too strongly and too bitterly, this had been his privilege as a prophet. In his prophetic rôle he had at once rediscovered the Gospel and delivered the Church from corruption and tyranny. The effects of his mission could be described in the words of the angel in the Apocalypse, 'Fallen, fallen is Babylon the great'. Luther would live on in accordance with his own prophecy: *Pestis eram vivus, moriens tua mors ero, Papa.*

Then in a valedictory oration Philip Melanchthon placed Luther in the succession of teachers who had preserved and renewed the Church: Isaiah, John the Baptist, Paul and Augustine. He had been a second Moses, sent against his own inclinations to lead God's people from the wilderness. He had always been a renovator, not an innovator. Like the rebuilders of Jerusalem in the days of Nehemiah, he had constructed the walls with one hand, and held the sword in the other; for while he had fought the enemies of true doctrine, he had simultaneously brought comfort to a host of burdened consciences with his spiritual writings and his German Bible. Amiable people had complained that Luther was too hard and rough in controversy. Yet his critics should remember the words of Erasmus, "God in these last days, in which great and terrible diseases have prevailed, has sent the world a harsh physician." In defending his doctrine, Luther had only obeyed his own conscience and had never acted with quarrelsome or spiteful intentions. And in eloquent though more commonplace terms, the eminent disciple listed the virtues of the master: his piety and continence, his readiness to compose the quarrels of others, his private kindliness, his hatred of intrigue and of lukewarmness, his singleness of purpose, his unfailing courage, his constant prayer and trust, his intellectual penetration and insight into human character, the breadth of his knowledge, his ability to use it in writing and lecturing, his outstanding gift of literary expression.

The phrases of Bugenhagen and Melanchthon were those of men overwhelmed by grief and loss. But they were spoken from the heart and without fear of contradiction before scores of people who knew Luther intimately; they were spoken by men who had felt the rigours of Luther's rule as well as the stimulus of his leadership. They were certainly inspired by a sense of occasion, by a sense of history, by the sure knowledge that they had lived in the presence of rare greatness.

The rites concluded, Luther's coffin was lowered into a grave just before the pulpit where he had so often preached. That this building has changed so markedly seems typical of almost all the places associated with Luther. The so-called ancestral home at Möhra was in fact built about 1618; the birthplace at Eisleben was burned about 1689; only a few fragments remain at the *bursa* of St. George in Erfurt, while the Augustinian church there was rebuilt from the ground over a century ago. Even the Black Cloister at Wittenberg has suffered grievously at the hand of the restorer, and many of the Luther-relics shown in the museums are of dubious authenticity. The spirit of the man lives in his writings, but it can hardly be sensed in the places he inhabited and made so famous throughout the world.

In some sense, Luther was fortunate to die a few months before the outbreak of a conflict which at the very least would have brought him exile and infinite distress, a conflict of which the unexpectedly mild outcome lay a good many years ahead. The Schmalkaldic War which erupted in the summer was marked by the incapacity of John Frederick and the other generals of the League. They mobilised with commendable speed and at first the odds seemed in their favour. In the late summer of 1546 the forces of Saxony, Hesse and the Protestant cities, a well-appointed army of more than 50,000 men with 110 pieces of artillery, marched into the Danube Valley. At Regensburg the troops at the Emperor's immediate disposal scarcely amounted to a fifth of this figure; the Duke of Bavaria naturally wavered, while in Bohemia Ferdinand had no success with his attempts to organise an attack upon Saxony. Retiring to Landshut, Charles was joined by a force of Spaniards and papal troops from Italy. During the September he recovered Regensburg and other towns in southern Germany, received major reinforcements from the Netherlands and frightened the cities of Ulm and Augsburg into withdrawing their contingents from the army of the League. Thanks largely to their own wrangling and needless delays, the Lutheran princes had now missed their first and best opportunity. As for the Emperor's ally Maurice of Saxony, he had so far prudently lain low, yet he now burst into the Ernestine lands and with Ferdinand's help conquered most of them in less than two months. In consequence of this new threat, though after anxious deliberations, the princes of the League agreed to divide their forces. Some 9,000 troops went to defend Württemberg and the Swabian cities, while others merely returned home. With the rest the corpulent but physically active John Frederick set off northward to recover his Saxon lands.

Despite the lateness of the season, the Emperor now bestirred his troops to eradicate the southern rebels. Swiftly he forced into surrender the Duke of Württemberg, the Swabian towns, and even the great cities of Augsburg, Frankfurt and Strassburg. Though he could not re-Catholicise them, he exacted huge fines, compelling them to admit his garrisons and renounce membership of the Schmalkaldic League. The Elector Palatine soon returned to his allegiance, while Catholicism was one more restored in Cologne. In Saxony, however, matters proceeded very differently. King Ferdinand was forced to retire by disaffection in Bohemia, and even among his own troops. John Frederick, recovering his grasp of the local situation, managed to overrun Albertine Saxony, including Weimar, Jena, Halle and other possessions of Maurice: had he boldly marched on into disloyal, Protestant Bohemia, things would have gone hard with the Habsburgs. In addition, King Francis again showed his hand to no small effect. He sent funds to the Elector and the Landgrave, engaged Swiss troops, stimulated the Turks to fresh hostilities and fanned the resentment of Pope Paul III against the Emperor. The latter was indeed already contending with the Papacy over the lordship of Parma and Piacenza. Unjustly believing Charles lukewarm in the struggle against heresy, the Pope recalled his troops to Italy on the plea that they had served for the agreed period.

Under these circumstances Charles decided to advance not directly into north Germany, but into Bohemia, where he could at once stabilise the kingdom and regroup his forces for an assault on Saxony. Joined in April 1547 by Ferdinand and Maurice at Tirschenreuth near the Bohemian Forest, he stood in command of 35,000 men, the formidable Duke of Alva being among his generals. Meanwhile the Elector John Frederick had failed to reunite with the Landgrave Philip or to preserve the initiative he had recently recovered. Philip stayed in the west, disposing his forces to ward off an attack upon Hesse from the Netherlands. From this point John Frederick could do nothing right. Quartering many of his troops elsewhere, he stood with about 9,000 at Meissen. His intelligence-system was so feeble that when Charles, Ferdinand and Maurice proceeded to invade Saxony, they were already almost facing him across the Elbe before he would believe they had reached the area. For a time he planned to withdraw upon Wittenberg; a sensible notion, since by delay and manoeuvre he might have assembled the forces at this moment being mustered by the north German princes and cities. Yet instead he encamped near Mühlberg, uncertain whether or not to dispute in force the crossing of the broad and swift-flowing river.

Arriving there on 24 April, the Emperor rejected the cautious counsels of Maurice and Alva and boldly ordered a crossing of the Elbe. His luck held. Unaware of his peril, John Frederick had sent ahead his artillery and made no serious effort to defend the high bank on his side, while fog concealed the initial moves of the Imperialists. Swimming and wading, the Spanish infantry seized the Elector's boats and constructed a bridge with them, as the Emperor in person, accompanied by cavalry and other light forces, crossed by a ford. As the sun penetrated the mist they found themselves in command of both banks and it was not long before the retreating Elector had to stand and fight amid the woods at Lochau. His main force broken early in the engagement, John Frederick tried with desperate personal courage to cut his way through the enemy at the head of a small detachment. Surrounded, exhausted and wounded in the face, he was at last obliged to surrender and go before his conqueror, whom he found in no magnanimous mood. Cutting him off in the middle of a submissive speech, the Emperor consigned him to the keeping of a Spanish general.

When Charles presently advanced on Wittenberg, he found the little capital defended by the Elector's wife, Isabella of Cleves. In order to force a rapid surrender, he showed a supreme disregard of Imperial law by sending his captive before a court-martial headed by Alva. This body immediately pronounced a sentence of death upon John Frederick. At first the latter refused to purchase his life by ordering Wittenberg to surrender, but the distressed entreaties of his family and subjects induced him to do so, and hence to accept the forfeiture of his electorate and most of his lands. Though Charles kept him imprisoned, John Frederick reasserted his dignity in a manner which would have moved Luther himself to admiration. With unswerving resolution he refused to buy his freedom and his lands by altering his faith, or by agreeing to abide by the future decisions of the General Council then in session.

When Charles entered Wittenberg in triumph, he pretended to feel displeasure even at the suspension of the Lutheran services. "They are mistaken", he said, "if they do this to give me pleasure. There has been no change of religion in other states, so why should there be any here?" He went up to the Castle Church and stood before Luther's tomb—a scene dramatic enough for any painter of histories! But when he was urged to disinter and dishonour the corpse of the heresiarch, his taste prevailed. "I make war not on the dead but upon the living; let him rest in peace; he is already before his judge." In later years, there spread a story that the Emperor's troops had in fact scattered Luther's remains, but in 1892 it was completely disproved when the tomb was reopened during restorations at the Castle Church.

The victorious Emperor, encouraged by the death of Francis I a few days before Mühlberg, proceeded to treat his living enemies with no great forbearance. Philip of Hesse had been shattered by the fall of his ally and accepted the mediation of the Elector of Brandenburg and of his own son-in-law Maurice of Saxony. These two princes offered solemn personal assurances that if Philip surrendered he should not be kept prisoner. Having agreed to demolish his fortresses, surrender his artillery, release his prisoners and pay a heavy fine, he was brought before the Emperor at Halle on 19 June and knelt to make humble confession of his offence. To his surprise he was then sent off to Alva's apartments, and despite the protests of the mediators kept in undignified captivity. Along with the former Elector John Frederick, he was transported from city to city in the Emperor's retinue and made a public spectacle. On the other hand, Charles had no intention of making Maurice omnipotent in and around Saxony. The Capitulation of 19 May had assigned to Maurice the *Kurkreis*, the province containing Wittenberg and accompanying the electoral office. Yet while he was invested with this dignity, his Ernestine relatives were not removed from the circle of the ruling princes. The Emperor allowed them to call themselves Dukes of Saxony and left them in possession of Weimar, Gotha, Eisenach and Coburg.

Amongst Luther's anxious disciples in Wittenberg the Emperor's coming had at first caused panic. Philip Melanchthon would have set off for Denmark, had the surrounding country not been filled with hostile troops. Katherine Luther and her family fled to Magdeburg; she returned to find her farm pillaged, but received help from the King of Denmark and other wealthy admirers of her late husband. In Wittenberg during the first dark days things indeed looked much worse than in fact they were. Maurice of Saxony, who had spent much of his boyhood in the courts of Albert of Mainz, Duke George and John Frederick, had no deep religious convictions. Yet he intended neither to undo Luther's work nor to obliterate its headquarters. He soon extended his protection to the congregations and professors; academic life settled down, and the terminal waves of students, ever renewed but ever much the same, passed through the lecture-halls which had lately echoed to Luther's voice.

For a few months it seemed that the Emperor stood on the brink of final triumph, but once again a host of fresh perils beset his schemes, and this time he failed to encounter them with outstanding ability or tact. A Burgundian-Netherlandish prince, but ever in process of becoming a Spaniard, Charles still lacked natural affinities with the German princes and people. Here he differed from his own dutiful brother Ferdinand, who understood the Germans and had won a certain popularity among them. From the viewpoint alone of his personal interest in the recovery of Hungary, Ferdinand could see the need for German loyalty. Such ambitions were hardly promoted by an Emperor who overthrew German princes with Spanish troops and who in due course planned to shower territories on his Spanish son Philip. Even the Catholic princes had no desire whatever to see Charles making and unmaking princes or turning a loose federation into an effective Imperial monarchy. The bonds uniting Pope and Emperor proved equally insecure. Charles had far less interest in rebuilding papal authority than in forcing practical reform upon the Church, a process which Ximenes had shown to be possible half a century earlier. But while Paul III had supported Charles against the Lutheran princes, he recoiled from the prospect of an overmighty Emperor controlling a General Council and leading a Catholic Reformation. He stoutly refused the Emperor's demands that all bishops should be compelled to reside in their dioceses and that Rome should cease appointing Italians to German benefices. Having opened the Council of Trent in 1545, he moved it in March 1547 into his own territory at Bologna, this much to the fury of Charles. While the latter's personal orthodoxy debarred substantial or permanent concessions to the Protestants, he was thus left with the whole task of pacifying German indignation and anticlericalism.

As a first step Charles issued in May 1548 the Interim of Augsburg, a document drawn up at his command by two moderate Catholic prelates and by Johann Agricola, still court chaplain to that prince of trimmers, Joachim II of Brandenburg. For the moment allowing clerical marriage and communion in both kinds, the Interim also dealt with the matter of justification in the phraseology of Regensburg. Otherwise, however, Protestant doctrine and worship were in effect proscribed. Hundreds of pastors—including Bucer himself, who ended his days in England—emigrated from the south German cities, upon which Charles could now impose heavy pressures. The Interim was binding only upon the Protestants, and the accompanying document which proposed the reform of a few of the worst abuses among the Catholic clergy did little to placate critical opinion. On the other hand, the Interim did not satisfy the Pope, for what looked to the Protestants a thinly disguised policy of persecution seemed to Paul III a bold essay in Caesaro-papalism. In Germany itself the responses were as usual dictated largely by local and secular interests. The great bankers and merchants of Augsburg and other southern cities had lent great sums to Charles; they also had important interests in the Habsburg Netherlands, in the New World, in Tyrolese and Hungarian mining. Even those who were not convinced Catholics had every reason to leave resistance to their social inferiors. The Fuggers and other banking families withdrew for a time from Augsburg to dissociate themselves from its Protestant policy, and hence preserve their own interests intact.

While the imprisoned John Frederick refused the Interim himself, poor Philip Melanchthon tried to see it as a basis for genuine compromise, and thus permanently damaged his reputation among the stauncher Lutherans. On the other hand, many northern princes like Albert of Prussia, John of Küstrin and John Albert of Mecklenburg took full advantage of their geographical position, from the first defying the Emperor and his Interim. They were supported by numerous northern cities, especially by the stout-hearted burghers of Magdeburg, where

Amsdorf, Luther's old comrade at Worms, linked up with the truculent historian and hebraist Flacius Illyricus to head a strong party of self-styled Genuine Lutherans (*Gnesio-Lutheraner*). These men roundly denounced the Philipists as temporisers, and they rallied that large element among the German people which had now forever divested itself of the Habsburg cult and had no intention of putting back the clock in matters of religion. Even so, the collapse of the Imperial programme owed less to this resurrection of Luther's defiant spirit than to the political restiveness of the princes, both Lutheran and Catholic. The Duke of Bavaria pointedly declined the Emperor's plan to form a close league of princes under Habsburg leadership. King Ferdinand, already chosen to succeed Charles on the Imperial throne, felt great offence when Charles suggested his own son Philip as Ferdinand's eventual successor. In this dispute, the princes greatly preferred Ferdinand's son Maximilian to the stiff young Spaniard, while the Electors sensed in Charles's plan the threat of a hereditary Empire and the loss of their electoral privileges. Again, even the Catholic princes did not relish the contemptuous manner in which Charles paraded his captive Philip of Hesse on his progresses. More important still, the unfortunate Philip was the father-in-law of Maurice, who had in addition other substantial causes for bitterness. His opportunism had yielded profits only at the expense of his Ernestine cousins, since the grudging Emperor had still not handed him the half-promised bishoprics of Magdeburg and Halberstadt. Not surprisingly, Maurice determined to change sides once again. In the autumn of 1551, along with the Hessian councillors, he came to an agreement with France, ratified in January 1552 by the new King Henry II as the Treaty of Chambord. In return for heavy cash-subsidies enabling him to mobilise against the Emperor, Maurice hereby agreed to assign to Henry's rule the French-speaking border cities of Metz, Verdun and Toul, which dominated Lorraine.

When the attack developed in the spring, the Emperor's power crumbled with amazing speed. The French seized the three cities; Bavaria stood neutral, while the disgruntled Ferdinand did little to help his brother. Marching south along with young William of Hesse, Maurice might have captured Charles himself but for a mutiny by one of his contingents. Wracked by gout, the Emperor was carried in a litter across the Brenner Pass to an ignominious safety. Yet even this dramatic triumph did not yield all the results desired by Maurice. The southern Protestant cities, the chief victims of the Interim, might now have been expected to throw their full weight into the scales against Charles. In fact they showed themselves anxious to avoid trouble and quite distrustful of Maurice. The latter had his own reasons to call for a pause. Now that the Emperor had freed the former Elector John Frederick, Maurice feared restive movements by the nobles at home in Saxony. He thus began to negotiate with King Ferdinand, whose interests proved far from incompatible with his own. At Passau in August 1552 the two arranged that the details of a permanent religious peace should be deferred to a future Diet, that the Interim should no longer be enforced, and that church lands already secularised should be left in the hands of their new owners. On the political front, they agreed that the German nation should be governed by its Diet, that foreign councillors and troops should be dismissed and Philip of Hesse set free. But while Maurice then moved to help Ferdinand in Hungary, the Emperor refused to implement the Passau treaty thus made over his head, and he resorted to further ill-advised expedients in order to recover power.

Not satisfied with returning to Germany and working for the succession of his son Philip, Charles took into his service the vilest adventurer thrown up by these disordered conditions. The Hohenzollern prince Albert Alcibiades, Margrave of Kulmbach-Bayreuth, had posed as a Protestant champion and at the same time as a German patriot resentful of the French alliance recently concluded by Maurice. He had collected a formidable force and started subjecting the cities and ecclesiastical princes of central Germany to ruthless pillaging and blackmail. Now enjoying the favour of Charles, he tried early in 1553 to extend his exploits into the north, thereby causing other princes to league against him regardless of their religious beliefs. Their task was somewhat lightened by the Emperor's withdrawal into the Netherlands after his failure to recapture Metz. In July the outrageous Albert Alcibiades suffered defeat at Sievershausen in Lüneburg, but in that bloody engagement Maurice himself, still only thirty-two years of age, received wounds which a couple of days later proved fatal. He was succeeded in the Electorate by his attractive brother August, a generous bene-factor of the university of Wittenberg and hence of Lutheranism itself.

Despite his gross opportunism, Maurice had ended by demon-strating that the Empire must grant recognition to the Pro-testants. His career had also afforded time for the rise of moderate and pacific attitudes among both Catholic and Pro-testant rulers. In default of genuinely liberal sentiments, war-weariness and a desire to restore secular order pointed the way to some sort of tolerance between the religious parties. Yet had Maurice happened to survive for a further two or three decades, the balance of power in Germany might have undergone radi-cal alteration, since in addition to his military and diplomatic enterprise, he was an able administrator who might have settled down and become one of the outstanding rulers of sixteenth-century Europe. Among all the princes who strove to build secular edifices upon the religious career of Luther, he seems the one most capable of breaking through the conservatism of the German state-system and of providing history with a more sophisticated alternative to that rather crude phenomenon of the future : the dominance of Hohenzollern Prussia.

From the turning-point of Sievershausen, the idea of a general settlement gradually prevailed over the sectional interests of the German powers. Preparing to abdicate and for the moment more concerned with imposing his son Philip upon England, the Emperor stood aside and allowed his brother a free hand to negotiate with the Protestants. The scene was that momen-tous Diet of Augsburg which opened in February 1555 and lasted over six months. From the beginning its deliberations ex-cluded all save Catholics and Lutherans. The Calvinist or Re-formed religion had as yet acquired little weight within the boundaries of the Empire, while all the major churches con-tinued to regard the Anabaptists and other sectarians as untouchables. Again, though the Lutherans wanted freedom of worship in Catholic states, and though some rulers were willing to extend a measure of tolerance to individuals, the same fear of chaos which had beset Luther continued to discourage hazardous experiments. The result of these general misgivings greatly benefited the Catholic cause, which had everything to lose by a *laissez-faire* policy on religion. The territories of most Catholic princes were becoming ever more deeply impregnated by Lutheranism, whereas on the other side the infant Counter-Reformation had as yet no hope of reconquering the Protestant north. The principle adopted at Augsburg—and subsequently labelled *cujus regio, ejus religio*—enabled each state to determine the religion of all its subjects. Dissenters were permitted to emigrate, accompanied by their wives and children; they should be allowed to sell their properties at a just price, but if still under personal servitude, they must purchase their release before departure. Each prince undertook not to proselytise abroad or to extend his protection to adherents of his own religion living in other states.

On the vexed matter of the secularised lands, the compromise at Augsburg again tended to favour the Catholic position. While all property secularised before the Treaty of Passau (1552) was to remain secularised, no further extension of this practice was to be allowed. In the outcome, some princes interpreted this clause to mean that they could still secularise bishoprics and monasteries within their own lands, so long as they respected the possessions of the prince-bishops and prince-abbots. Ferdinand himself stood adamant against any demand that ecclesiastical princes should be allowed to embrace Protestantism. On this point the declaration at Augsburg took the form not of an agreement but of an Imperial decree. It stated that should such princes take this step, their electing chapters would have the immediate right to elect a Catholic successor. This decree, known as the *reservatio ecclesiastica*, soon became a perennial source of political and legal disputes. What, for example, should happen when a whole chapter turned Protestant and elected a Protestant prince-bishop? Ferdinand's struggle to maintain the ecclesiastical reservation led him to make one significant concession to the Protestants, though he made it in a confidential document and not among the public acts of the Diet of Augsburg. In effect it allowed those nobles and towns within ecclesiastical states which had already turned Protestant to continue so without actual molestation. Nevertheless, his efforts did not go unrewarded in subsequent history. Despite all the difficulties of interpretation, despite the straining of its provisions by many intriguers, the reservation did much to preserve the surviving ecclesiastical states for the rest of the life of the Holy Roman Empire. When erelong the Counter-Reformation arrived in force, these states provided many of its most important bases, and the reservation thus bulks large in the history of German and Austrian Catholicism.

The obvious limitations of Augsburg and the appalling collapse of its system in the Thirty Years War have often been allowed to obscure the impressive degree of good sense and realism evinced by most of its provisions. The negotiators of 1555—they were mainly officials and not princes in person—could hardly be expected to provide for unforeseen future events like the rise of Calvinist states in the Empire, or to guard in advance against the follies of seventeenth-century politicians who failed to work in the same spirit. If their decisions were dictated by political realism rather than by modern ideals of toleration, they nevertheless mark one step in the direction of these ideals. It was no small matter that Catholic Emperors and princes should accord organised heresy a legal status within the framework of the Empire. It might indeed be claimed that Luther's contemporaries learned the first lesson more quickly than their successors were to learn the subsequent ones. And if the Lutheran states were to contribute less than the Calvinists to the defence of Protestantism, in their stodgy pacifism they contributed far more to that slow building of confidence by which the later lessons of toleration were gradually to be taught.

However uneasy, however often punctuated by disputes, the truce that lasted from the Peace of Augsburg to the Defenestration of Prague (1618) was a long one. It gave Lutheranism time to compose its internal quarrels, Calvinism time to establish a foothold in the Empire, sectarianism time to demonstrate its peaceable character. Still more strikingly, it allowed German Catholicism time to draw upon the spiritual resources of the Counter-Reformation, for the latter was essentially an Italian and a Spanish creation and needed several decades to adapt itself to the German idiom. While Germany was about to receive these influences, in 1556 she at least got rid of an exotic factor far less easy to assimilate: the increasingly Spanish flavour of Habsburg rule as represented by Charles V, whose multi-national heritage became a curse to all the lands it comprised, even to Spain herself. From Augsburg at least until the reign of the Spanish-trained Rudolph II (1576–1612), there occurred something in the nature of a Habsburg new deal. Luther did not in fact usher in an era of stark tragedy. Culturally and intellectually the Germans had much to gain as well as much to lose from the diversification of their religious life. Given later on a little more princely wisdom and a firmer organisation to resist meddlesome foreign powers, the Germans need not have paid for their new opportunities so terrible a price as the Thirty Years War.

We have already suggested that the direct influence of the Reformation made for the aggrandisement of landowning aristocracies rather than for that of the princes. The rise of territorial states—in other words, the success of partnerships between princes and aristocracies—seems a process characteristic of the fifteenth and sixteenth centuries as a whole. Begun before Luther's time, it would doubtless have continued even had Luther never existed. On the other hand, the Reformation as consolidated in the Augsburg settlement helped to create among the rulers of Germany new party divisions, based at first (though later to a decreasing extent) upon religious differences. These divisions in turn helped, along with other factors of longer standing, to inhibit any revival of the Holy Roman Empire as a working confederation of likeminded rulers and cities. The narrowly-defeated attempt by Ferdinand II and Wallenstein to reassert Habsburg hegemony shows that Augsburg had not totally destroyed that possibility. Yet the foundations of confidence among the princes and cities in the Imperial dynasty had been shaken by the Reformation and by no means firmly restored by the Augsburg compromise. Worldly as were most of the princes, they could not remain unaffected by a partisanship based on religion and on the need to defend the material changes accomplished during the crisis of 1520–55. As for the cities of central Europe, the weak and vacillating policy shown by many during the final stages of that crisis served to enhance the decline in reputation and power already brought upon them by economic forces. For a host of reasons the centre of European gravity was moving to the west, to the north, to the states and cities on the Baltic, the North Sea and the Atlantic.

Could Luther himself have returned to witness the terms of Augsburg and the world they created, he would doubtless have felt deep disappointment at this apparent outcome of his struggle. Long before the end of his life he had been forced into compromises between his early glorification of the free conscience and the subsequent demands of a torn and precariously balanced world. But this mechanised, large-scale forcing of consciences, this attempt to finalise religious frontiers, this apotheosis of the State, would have seemed to him at best the bitterest of necessities imposed in the face of a victory no more than half gained. Luther's critics all too often forget that he no more fought for a divided Christendom than did his opponents. Moreover, he would doubtless have reflected that Augsburg had sealed off large areas of central Europe already in part converted to his gospel and perhaps with a little more effort to be won in their entirety. The Catholic rulers, soon to be reinforced by the decisions of the Council of Trent and by the Jesuits, had now been handed the legal instruments to repress a Protestantism which still looked capable of spontaneous advances, still able to yield profits in a free market. In the years which followed, those who retained anything of Luther's idealism might have been pardoned for thinking that the Word had rolled across Germany like a mighty tidal wave, but only to recede as swiftly, leaving the Evangelical religion awash in a patchwork of stagnant little pools. It took many decades to show Lutherans that the actual situation was less depressing than this, that the battle was half won as well as half lost, that their religion would form a permanent influence on the history of the German people, on the history of Christianity throughout the world.

Chapter Eight

The Sequels: Luther in Retrospect

TWO years after Augsburg a Venetian ambassador reported to his government that nine-tenths of Germany was Protestant. Though neither he nor anyone else could accurately employ such vulgar fractions, the detailed evidence goes some way to justify his statement. When the Palatinate lands had been taken over to Lutheranism by the Elector Otto-Henry in 1556–7, the only considerable Catholic enclave in central Germany was formed by the ecclesiastical principalities of Bamberg, Würzburg and Mainz. Even here the towns and the aristocracy had in large part defected. So they had also throughout much of Bavaria, Austria and the southern bishoprics of Salzburg and Augsburg. In the seventies, the Emperor was to grant the privilege of Lutheran household worship to the nobles of Austria, Styria and Carinthia. In the north-west the surviving Catholic bishoprics of Münster, Paderborn and Cologne might well have collapsed but for the resolute pressures of the Habsburg government in the nearby Netherlands. Apart from some small areas belonging to the prelates of Mainz and Hildesheim, the whole of northern Germany east of the Weser was solidly Protestant. So were nearly all the universities of the region, with their steadily growing output of Lutheran pastors.

The rise of Calvinism and of the Counter-Reformation modified this situation more slowly and less radically than is sometimes supposed. Duke Albert V of Bavaria founded the Jesuit college at Ingolstadt in 1556 and established the Order at Munich three years later. But the influence of the Jesuits outside the Habsburg and Wittelsbach lands only began to be significant during the sixties, when from Mainz and Speyer they strove to dominate the Rhineland. As a popular movement, Calvinism emerged from the Netherlands and developed only in parts of the northern Rhineland and Westphalia. But in 1563 the Elector Frederick III took the Palatinate into the Reformed camp and made Heidelberg its main intellectual centre in Germany. Despite a Lutheran intermission in 1576–83, this state assumed the political leadership of German Calvinism and ended by precipitating the Thirty Years War. The small principalities of Anhalt and Nassau—the latter under the House of Orange—also turned Calvinist and so did the major but remote municipality of Bremen. Later on there were a few princely converts who did not carry with them many of their subjects: such was the grandfather of the Great Elector, John Sigismund of Brandenburg, who became a Calvinist in 1613. On the other hand, the strength of German loyalty to Luther appears from the fact that Calvinism proved unable to establish its distinctive ecclesiastical and political patterns. Not unjustly, the churches in these Reformed lands have been dubbed Lutheran churches professing Calvinist creeds. Even so, from the mid-century hatred grew harsher between the Evangelical and the Reformed; even the impassive Calvin so far forgot himself as to call the Lutherans ministers of Satan. The relationship was made no easier by the fact that Philipism—already called Crypto-Calvinism by the orthodox—formed a bridge which carried many Lutherans over to the Reformed faith.

In the event the continuance of this internal dispute mattered more to Luther's churches than did the erosions of the Calvinists. The initial favours of the Elector August of Saxony (1553–86) gave strength to Philipism in Saxony and Thuringia, but by 1574 he began to fear that its over-zealous leaders might involve him in Calvinism. Such misgivings led him to join those who were urging reunion within the body of Lutheranism and he took a major part in the negotiations surrounding the Formula of Concord. This document, first drawn up in 1577 by Martin Chemnitz and other theologians, became the Lutheran equivalent to the Catholic decrees of Trent. It refused to accept some positions demanded by the fanatical Flacius Illyricus, yet on the main issues it did not compromise with Philipism. It declared the Scriptures the sole criterion of dogma. Man's total depravity since the Fall was explicitly stated, though the logical Calvinist deduction of double predestination to salvation and reprobation was denied. Likewise no loophole was left for the introduction of Calvinist teaching on the eucharist. The Formula was joined with the three Creeds, the Augsburg Confession of 1530, the Schmalkaldic Articles of 1537 and Luther's two Catechisms, to make up the Book of Concord. The latter then found surprisingly general acceptance and was signed in 1580 or soon afterwards by 51 princes, 35 cities and over 8,000 pastors. This movement together with a general decline of Philipism restored internal order and created a hitherto unknown decree of uniformity, yet it broadened the gulf which divided the Lutherans from the predominantly Calvinist Protestantism of western Europe. Even a few recalcitrant Evangelical states, notably Denmark, refused to accept the Book of Concord, and throughout the Lutheran world it never attained the authority of the Augsburg Confession.

The century that followed has inevitably been labelled the Age of Orthodoxy. Under the leadership of Melanchthon's former pupil Chemnitz, the German Evangelical churches rejected the doctrine of Synergism and other Philipist attempts to dilute Luther's doctrine. But they restored Luther's letter without restoring his spirit. They also continued to respect Melanchthon as a philosopher, while his work as a humanist educator and his revival of Aristotle remained paramount influences in the Lutheran schools and universities. The Age of Orthodoxy tried to follow up Luther's creative age by a process of cataloguing and arranging; it sought to protect the germ of faith by a thick husk of logic. If rank-and-file Lutherans were not bored to death, this must have been largely due to the distinguished succession of musicians and hymnologists at work in their midst throughout the two hundred years following Luther's death.

During the later decades of the seventeenth century the Pietist movement, led by the Alsatian Philipp Jakob Spener (d. 1705), pushed back the frontiers of Orthodoxy. Pietism shows obvious affinities not only with the Moravian Brethren but with English Methodism; it was through this movement rather than through his own formal theology that Luther influenced John Wesley. But if Luther would have applauded the efforts of Spener and his groups (known as *collegia pietatis*) to spread a heartfelt religion, he would certainly have detested some of their theological tendencies. The Pietists showed little regard for his 'extrinsic' version of justification by faith; instead they stressed practical Christianity and like Augustine spoke of justification through righteous living, through becoming righteous rather than through the undeserved imputation of Christ's righteousness. Some of them demanded a set pattern of conversion-experiences and supposed that these qualified a man for acceptance by God.

Yet whatever may be thought of its theology or of its narrow-minded Puritanism, the movement has a great place in German religious history. It not only terminated the Age of Orthodoxy but erected barriers against the coming tide of Rationalism, which never swept away its devotional traditions. The University of Halle, dominated from 1692 by Spener's famous disciple August Hermann Francke (d. 1727), sent out missions to India, and it inspired the reorganisation of the swift-growing Lutheran bodies of colonial America by their patriarch Henry Melchior Muhlenberg (d. 1787). Francke's own schools, orphanages, hospitals and bible-publishing activities in north Germany echoed the practical zeal of Luther's later years.

The relation of J. S. Bach to the conflict between Orthodoxy and Pietism must arouse the interest of historians, since Bach was a deeply engaged Lutheran and by any sensible definition the greatest Evangelical Christian of his age. He was reared in the shadow of the Wartburg at Eisenach, where two centuries earlier the schoolboy Luther had sung for pence. The solid, pious cantor and family man, so little known in his day outside Saxony, wrote in and for the Evangelical Church: at the head of a manuscript he would pen the words *Soli Deo Gloria*, and he would pray for the guidance of Christ before he began to write. Like so much of the art of the Baroque Age, Catholic and Protestant, his music yields more to those who by experience, or at least by some act of imagination, can share the religious emotions at its heart. But even church-musicians use a language other than that of philosophy and theology. As Bach expounded the great Christian truths, he viewed the strife of verbal partisans as a worrying irrelevance. He was of neither party but in some sense he comprehended both. While the form and theological emphases of his cantatas are in line with Orthodoxy, it seems by no means fanciful to associate their emotional content, their sense of a profound devotion to the person of Christ, with the Pietism of his age.

Before the death of Bach a third force had begun to intrude upon the Lutheran world: that of Rationalism, prominently represented in Halle itself by the mathematician and philosopher Christian Wolff (d. 1754). Making God an abstraction, Jesus a moralist and St. Paul an adulterator of the simple ethical message, the extremer rationalists shifted completely outside Luther's orbit. Two aspects of the Enlightenment nevertheless proved fruitful in relation to Evangelical thought. In its train came the philosophical revival associated with the great names of Kant and Hegel; though not specifically Christian, it brought fresh concepts into the world of theology. More important still were new modes of biblical criticism which might have fascinated Luther by their methods yet would have troubled him by some of their conclusions. Their origins can in fact be traced back at least to Johann Bengel (d. 1752), who adopted the method of grouping New Testament manuscripts into genealogical trees. Subsequently J. S. Semler (d. 1791) investigated with the eye of a comparative historian the growth of Jewish and Christian doctrine, and he ended by stressing the relatively low historical value of some of the Scriptural books.

The pietistic reactions stirred up by these and other developments culminated in the third centennial celebrations of 1817, when Claus Harms, amid widespread applause, published his ninety-five theses against rationalist apostasy. In that same year the Kingdom of Prussia (later followed by other German states) forced the Lutheran and the Reformed Churches into amalgamation, thus arousing a major movement of secession and the rise of 'free' Lutheran congregations. The latter rejected all forms of state-control and until 1840 suffered a mild persecution by the governments concerned. Thenceforth the mere ecclesiastical and political history of nineteenth-century Lutheranism both in Germany and in America seems a tiresome story of schisms, feuds and negotiations, yet these external features should not be allowed to hide a continuing religious vitality. It is also true that between 1817 and the rise of Hitler the Evangelical churches failed to breathe the spirit of freedom into the German body politic. Yet that this failure arose from German secular conditions rather than from the inherent defects of Lutheranism is suggested by at least three historical examples: the development of 'model' democracies in all the Scandinavian Lutheran states; the democratic, even factious stirring of the Evangelical communities in America; the firm and often heroic resistance of many Lutheran leaders in Nazi Germany. This last crude and opportunist tyranny did at least give German Lutheranism the chance to throw off inhibiting social and political traditions; despite some temporisers and renegades, it accomplished this feat to its lasting honour.

On the more narrowly devotional and intellectual fronts the vitality of these churches has never been in question during the last 150 years. The religious life of a Lutheran congregation is not much dependent upon institutional centralisation and the turmoil of this period has only served to display the durable character of Martin Luther's legacy. Alongside the elements of hypocrisy and self-deception found amid all forms of institutional religion, it has been a period of missions, of a rising social conscience, of great philosophers, theologians and historians, of extending intellectual horizons, of more liberal and receptive attitudes toward other forms of religion. If modern Protestantism has tended to demolish its internal walls, to become one world instead of many, one of the causes lies in a reviving concern for the work of the original Reformers, especially for the ideas of Luther.

The term 'Luther Renaissance' is often applied to the writings of the Swedes since 1900 and to relatively recent manifestations like the publication of Karl Holl's collected essays in 1927. In essence, however, a deeper understanding of Luther's religion and a growing dependence of Protestant theology upon its direct study can be traced back at least to the time of Søren Kierkegaard (d. 1855). Both independently and through Kierkegaard, Luther even became one of the ancestors of Christian existentialism, the way of thought which rejects moralism and intellectualism and sees life as a crisis involving the total person. Again, in our own century Karl Barth, Emil Brunner and others evolved their dialectical theology in large part on the basis of Luther's theocentricity, his paradoxes, his doctrine of the Word. And it is significant that these two leaders were trained in the Calvinist tradition, and that, having drunk just as deeply at the Lutheran springs, they then dominated for many years the whole of non-Catholic religious thinking.

Luther's most obvious and undisputed achievement was the founding of the Lutheran churches and their inspiration through many vicissitudes, some of which saw the decline, others the recrudescence of his spirit. These perennial influences have arisen not merely from the more intellectual aspects of his theology—which have been increasingly shared with non-Lutheran Protestants—but also from certain very tangible and practical legacies. Did any religious reformer produce such a range of literary instruments for his congregations? Luther gave them a great vernacular Bible, a liturgy, two remarkable catechisms, a new sort of hymn-book, a huge collection of standard sermons, a whole literature of apologetics. In our final pages we propose to revert to broader themes and stress some far more debatable aspects of Luther's career and personality: his share in this greatest of Christian schisms; his rôle as 'hero of the German nation'; his renovation of Christian social teaching.

Luther's assault upon Rome and upon the doctrinal bases of her authority have a deeper significance than his assault on concrete abuses, and of this he was well aware.

John Huss attacked and castigated only the Pope's evil and scandalous life, but I have attacked the Pope's doctrine and overthrown him.

He struck at a doctrinal system and at a concept of authority from which, in his view, abuses sprang as a matter of course. Historians have much to say on indulgences, justification, and other early issues of the revolt. They then tend to assume that his swift, violent, final slamming of the door on the Papacy came as an inevitable consequence—so inevitable as to need little comment or explanation. Yet was not this particular step far more controversial, more instinctive, taken more blindly, than any other of his career? The milder men came much more gradually to the last cleavage of the ways; they reached it with some foreboding, some lingering regrets. Yet Luther made the break with passion and something approaching alacrity; he made it almost at the outset of his career as a Reformer. Thenceforth he never looked back, and the very thought of the Papacy aroused in his breast an even deeper, more unassuageable hatred.

This ruthless decision cannot be defended on the ground that Luther shrewdly predicted its results; he was not a prophet in the sense that he foresaw the future religious contours of Europe. He thought of the Papacy not merely as heretical but as moribund; he saw himself as the unworthy instrument of a divine plan for reordering the structure and teaching of the whole Christian Church. He supposed that the experience of recent centuries proved that no real reforms could possibly come from Rome; this not because of mere personal and administrative flaws, but because the Papacy and the whole hierarchy, abandoned by God, were bound to maintain a manifestly erroneous and heretical version of the Christian religion. The neuroses, the obsessions, above all the miscalculations involved in his attitude can easily enough be censured or pitied. To his death Luther bore the wounds of a Prometheus who had once dared to pit his frail resources against the huge and hoary powers of institutional Christendom. He was a combatant by nature, still more through agonising experience, yet owning also a deep sensitivity, he took the painful consequences. Not for a moment should he be discussed as if he were coolly weighing the issues in the comfort of a twentieth-century study.

Upon his intractable violence moral judgments are not necessarily inappropriate, yet they have too often come from minds unfree to reconsider the basic issues, or guided by unrealistic erudition. Fr. Denifle, for example, proved nothing against Luther's intellectual integrity when he cited passages from medieval theologians, mostly unknown to Luther, in order to

indicate that justification by faith had always been the teaching
of the Catholic Church. Quite apart from the fact that Luther's
imputatory doctrine modified this tradition, his reproaches were
directed less at academic Christianity than at the real Church
of recent centuries, a Church seemingly all too hard at work to
set forth the very reverse of justification by faith. Luther's criticism of this Church—however little he understood its surviving
potentialities—made good sense to millions of people. Had he
not been talking about a real situation he could hardly have
convulsed European society. Again, it seems less than convincing to censure his impatience simply on the ground that, not
long afterwards, the Papacy did achieve a striking measure of
self-reform and Church-reform. In 1520 this was a long-
awaited and seemingly most improbable miracle. Moreover,
that it really happened was due in no inconsiderable measure
to the terrifying stimulus of Luther's own career. Yet again,
these laudable reforms did not in the event secure the Pauline
re-emphasis which Luther and his party supposed to be the
minimum basis for an authentic Christianity. Had they all lived
on to read the decrees of Trent, Luther would have been able
to turn on his milder friends and say, "I told you so from the
first. This is not the Evangelical religion for which we have
fought; by her very nature Rome cannot give us the Gospel."

In this imaginary situation, the thoughts of a man like Philip
Melanchthon might nevertheless have gone back to Regensburg
in 1541; he might well have wondered whether Luther's anti-
Roman ferocity had not doomed in advance the ecumenical
aspirations of Catholics like Contarini and Gropper. Had
Luther left the door slightly ajar during the previous twenty
years, might there not have been at least a better chance of a
tolerable re-union, based upon a Pauline-Augustinian reorienta-
tion within the whole Church? But if for his part Luther had
foreseen the permanent divisions which arose from his un-
compromising policy, he might nevertheless have preferred
them to this alternative. If confronted by the agonising choice,
would he not rather have seen a portion of Europe following
the Evangelical faith than all Europe permeated by a heavily-
diluted version of that faith? Yet we may well doubt whether

at any stage history did in fact offer these two alternatives. Even had Luther behaved with much greater moderation and charity toward Rome, it seems improbable that during the crucial decades Rome would have been captured by the ideals of Contarini. This would have been a second and even more unlikely Roman miracle!

Luther was a man of religion and any attempt to present him in other terms is foredoomed to failure. His contributions to secular life were for the most part indirect and remain difficult to assess with accuracy. His criticisms of the economic world were ethical, their effects imponderable. And as we have argued, his political doctrines did not greatly affect the internal trends of the Lutheran states, whether autocratic or constitutional. Yet for a moment as brief as it was wonderful, he stood at the head of a German nation united at least in the grievances he had so memorably expressed. Even today his writings appear a landmark in the ethnic and cultural consciousness of German-speaking people. Nevertheless this great rôle might easily have been greater still: the outcome is apt to seem an anticlimax when the possibilities are envisaged. With the cooperation of the Emperor he might well have united the Teutons in one religion. In the event this rising national consciousness did not meet with a monarchy which could use it to advance German political unity. It collided with something more than the firm religious principles of the dogged Habsburg ruler. It collided with Charles's private dream of a world still ruled by an Emperor to whom the Pope was a necessary if junior partner; a Ghibbeline world worthy of Dante's *De Monarchia*. Still more important, it collided with the outlook of a cosmopolitan dynast, one withdrawn ever further from the German nation by the Spanish heritage. Personalities apart, Luther met the Habsburgs at one of the least receptive moments of their history. Contrary to the aims of its sponsors, the Lutheran Reformation thus tore northern Germany apart not merely from the Habsburgs but from the whole concept of Empire. Moreover, by gradual stages north German separatism found its political centre not in landlocked Saxony, not in the westward-looking Hanseatic lands, but in Brandenburg-Prussia, a military frontier-state better fitted to use the negative than the creative aspects of Luther's legacy.

On the other hand, within the wide borderlands between religion and social philosophy, Luther's ideas proved fresh and invigorating; they must be taken seriously as a force at work within the emergent societies of Protestant Europe. In those days church and society were mutually pervasive: Luther could not change the former without in some degree changing also the latter. That seemingly provocative notion 'the priesthood of all believers' exerted a pacifying influence upon society. In replacing the concept of juridical and mediatorial hierarchy by one of popular education and congregational fellowship, Luther allayed anticlericalism, since, in a time of advancing lay knowledge, clericalism and anticlericalism naturally battened upon each other. To raise the layman—even the lay woman—from being a second-class citizen of the Church was indeed to remove one menacing threat to the Church. The more secular aspect of this change was Luther's insistence upon the sacredness of all callings, even the most humble and physical. It still retains a profound appeal, and one to which our present essay has so far failed to do justice.

> What you do in your house is worth as much as if you did it up in heaven for our Lord God. . . . It looks a great thing when a monk renounces everything and goes into a cloister, carries on a life of asceticism, fasts, watches, prays, etc. . . . On the other hand it looks a small thing when a maid cooks and cleans and does other housework. But because God's command is there, even such a small work must be praised as a service of God far surpassing the holiness and asceticism of all monks and nuns, for here there is no command of God.

Even though these ideas have come to English-speakers in a famous hymn of George Herbert, they remain Luther's ideas. In the early sixteenth-century context they were bold and truly epoch-making departures. Within them there lay ideals of family life and social relations which both attracted and moulded the townsmen, the professional people, the lesser landowners, the middle orders which were simultaneously laying hold upon the economic, social and intellectual activities of Europe. Luther's social-religious teaching did not, however, stop at this level. He constantly imparted the ideal of disinterested labour in the service of all one's fellow men, the notion that service and vocation are manifold and embrace the relations between husband and wife, parent and child, shopkeeper and customer, master and servant, ruler and people. Ironically, this alleged despiser of good works stands far nearer to modern notions of beneficence than does any man of his age —with the possible exception of the humanitarians in the new Italian religious orders. For Luther service links with faith, because social solidarity is based on common belief and because the man inwardly stabilised by faith can be truly free to devote his energies to others. In his phraseology of 1520, a Christian man can become 'servant to all' just because he has already become a 'free lord' in the realm of the spirit. Beneficence can no longer be based on the calculation that it gets one into heaven.

In the last resort Luther's place in history must largely be assessed in relation to his conscious objective: the renovation of religious life and thought. In a responsible spirit he pursued the task of a biblical specialist intent to revive the original Gospel and make it fully meaningful to ordinary men and women. He conceived that the core of the Gospel lay in some such propositions as these: that the inner being and intentions of God cannot be deduced by our limited minds from the natural world, or from the normal experiences of mankind; that philosophical theology can open up no significant relations with God; that mystical 'states' resulting from spiritual athleticism remain unreliable guides; that men cannot be made acceptable by personal virtues, by proxy, through saints or other human middle-men; that the whole of the faith-giving and reconciling process comes from the side of God and through no other agency save Jesus Christ.

Luther hated to hear his churches called Lutheran, since he believed himself called not to found a new Church but to revitalise a deeply ailing Catholic Church in the light of documented primitive Christianity. This humanist and Protestant watchword *ad fontes* covers only a part of his message, yet it often lends weight to his dogmatism and helps to palliate the error of his expectations. One should think of him as a positive Evangelical rather than as a negative Protestant; and whereas the term Evangelical has since come to suggest an emotional religion, in his day and his mind it implied a highly rational return to the Gospel documents. The fidelity of his own reasoning and intuitions to the recorded thought of Jesus and Paul cannot become a theme of our present essay. Yet one might reasonably claim that Luther's permanent distinction lies in his powerful striving toward this fidelity rather than in the more imaginative and personal flights of his thought. He approached the sources with the mind of a theologian rather than with that of a historian, but to this day he captures the hearts of those who regard a historical approach as essential to any solid and lasting revival of the Christian religion.

Additional Reading

The following brief list is limited to works available in English. It should be viewed alongside the fact that one bibliography of the Reformation-period in Germany alone occupies seven large volumes! Many of the following have useful short bibliographies, notably the two by R. H. Bainton. The dates given are those of the first edition; more recently a number of these books have become available as paperbacks, marked [P] below.

Causes and Background of the Reformation

Bainton, R. H., *The Reformation of the Sixteenth Century* (1953). [P]

Brandi, K., *The Emperor Charles V* (1939). [P]

Chadwick, O., *The Reformation* (1964). [P]

Cohn, N., *The Pursuit of the Millennium* (1957). [P]

Dickens, A. G., *Reformation and Society in Sixteenth Century Europe* (1966). [P]

Elton, G. R., *Reformation Europe 1517–1559* (1963). [P]

Hurstfield, J., and others, *The Reformation Crisis* (1965). [P]

Léonard, E. G., *A History of Protestantism: I. The Reformation* (1966).

Mackinnon, J., *The Origins of the Reformation* (1939).

Grimm, H. J., *The Reformation Era, 1500–1650* (New York and London, 1954, revised 1965). [P]

Williams, G. H., *The Radical Reformation* (1962).

The German Reformation

Carsten. F. L., *Princes and Parliaments in Germany* (1959).

Eells, H., *Martin Bucer* (New Haven, 1931).

Hildebrandt, F., *Melanchthon: Alien or Ally?* (1946).

Holborn, H., *A History of Modern Germany, The Reformation* (1965).

Ranke, L. von, *History of the Reformation in Germany* (3 vols., 1845–7).

On Carlstadt see E. G. Rupp in *Journal of Theological Studies*, x (1959), and on Müntzer the same author in *Bulletin of the John Rylands Library*, xliii (1961), and lxxxviii (1966).

The Reformation in other Countries

Clebsch, W. A., *England's Earliest Protestants. 1520–1535* (New Haven, London, 1964).

Dickens, A. G., *The English Reformation* (1964). [P]

Donaldson, G., *The Scottish Reformation* (1960).

Dunkley, E. H., *The Reformation in Denmark* (1948).

Fox, P., *The Reformation in Poland* (1924).

Parker, T. M., *The English Reformation to 1558* (1950). [P]

Potter, G. R., ch. vi–viii in E. Bonjour, H.S. Offler and G. R. Potter, *A Short History of Switzerland* (1952).

Rupp, E. G., *The Making of the English Protestant Tradition* (1947).

Wendel, F., *Calvin. The Origins and Development of his Religious Thought* (1963).

Luther: Biographical

Bainton, R. H., *Here I Stand: A Life of Martin Luther* (1950). [P]

Boehmer, H., *Luther and the Reformation in the Light of Modern Research* (1930).

Boehmer, H., *Road to Reformation* (Philadelphia, 1946).

Fife, R. H., *The Revolt of Martin Luther* (New York, 1957).

Green, V. H. H., *Luther and the Reformation* (1964).

Grimm, H. J., *Luther and Melanchthon* (Philadelphia, 1961).

Köstlin, J., *Life of Luther* (1883).

Lau, F., *Luther* (1963).

Mackinnon, J., *Luther and the Reformation* (4 vols., 1925–30).

Ritter, G., *Luther his Life and Work* (1963).

Rupp, E. G., *Luther's Progress to the Diet of Worms* (1951). [P]

Schwiebert, E. G., *Luther and his Times* (St. Louis, 1950).

Todd, J. M., *Martin Luther, A Biographical Study* (1964).

Luther: Thought and Theology

McDonough (below) has a good up-to-date bibliography on Luther's theology.

Allen, J. W., 'Luther's Political Conceptions' in *Tudor Studies presented to A. F. Pollard* (1924).

Bornkamm, H., *Luther's World of Thought* (St. Louis, 1958).

Carlson, E. M., *The Reinterpretation of Luther* (1948).

Cranz, F. E., *The Development of Luther's Thought on Justice, Law and Society* (Cambridge, Mass., 1959).

Headley, J. M., *Luther's View of Church History* (New Haven and London, 1963).

McDonough, T. M., *The Law and the Gospel in Luther* (1963).

Reu, M., *Luther and the Scriptures* (1944).

Rupp, E. G., *The Righteousness of God* (1953).

Saarnivaara, U., *Luther Discovers the Gospel* (St. Louis, 1951).

Watson, P. S., *Let God be God: An Interpretation of the Theology of Martin Luther* (1947).

Wood, A. S., *Luther's Principle of Biblical Interpretation* (1960).

Luther's Successors: Lutheranism

Drummond, A. L., *German Protestantism since Luther* (1951).

Pauck, W., *The Heritage of the Reformation* (Glencoe, Illinois; Boston, 1950).

Pelikan, J., *Obedient Rebels* (1964).

Swihart, A. K., *Luther and the Lutheran Church* (1961).

Whale, J. S., *The Protestant Tradition* (1955). [P]

Luther's Works: Select Documents

The standard Weimar edition of Luther's works, begun in 1883 and to be completed about 1970, will include 57 vols. of his original writings, 12 vols. of his German Bible, 11 of his letters and 6 of the *Table Talk*. The American Edition (St. Louis and Philadelphia, ed. J. Pelikan and H. T. Lehmann) will contain

55 vols. when completed. The following have texts in English, apart from Kidd, who does not translate the Latin documents.

Atkinson, J., *Luther: Early Theological Works* (Library of Christian Classics. xvi, 1962).

Dillenberger, J., *Martin Luther. Selections from his Writings* (New York, 1961). [P]

Elton, G. R., *Renaissance and Reformation, 1300–1648* (New York, London, 1963).

Hillerbrand, H. J., *The Reformation in its Own Words* (1964).

Kidd, B. J., *Documents Illustrative of the Continental Reformation* (1911).

Packer, J. I., and Johnston, O. R., *Martin Luther on the Bondage of the Will* (1957).

Pauck, W., *Luther: Lectures on Romans* (Library of Christian Classics, xv, 1961).

Smith, P., and Jacobs, C. M., *Luther's Correspondence* (2 vols. 1913–18).

Tappert, T. G., *Luther: Letters of Spiritual Counsel* (Library of Cristian Classics, xviii, 1955).

Wace, H., and Buchheim, C. A., *Primary Works* (1896).

Woolf, B. L., *Reformation Writings of Martin Luther* (1952).

Index

INDEX

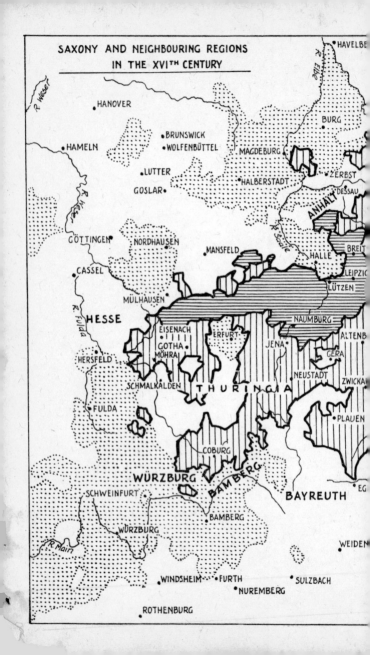